LIVING IN MAURITIUS

Pages 6-7: *The bright red flowers of the flame trees stand out against a landscape of calm blue-grey and discreet green.*

Pages 8-9: *Many houses and places in Mauritius have names that are evocative of distant shores. Verdun, at Beau Bassin, has a glazed verandah that exudes light, air and elegance.*

Pages 10-11: *Port-Louis teems with activity. The small shops are as picturesque as they are numerous.*

Translated from the French by Isabelle Desvaux de Marigny and Henriette Valentin Lagesse

First published in Mauritius in 1991 by
Les Nouvelles Editions du Pacifique, 77, rue du Cherche Midi, 75006 Paris
Reprinted 1992, 1994

Copyright © 1990 Editions Didier Millet/
Les Editions du Pacifique

Library of Congress Catalog Card Number 90-70388

All Rights Reserved. No part of this publication may be reproduced or transmitted in any form or by any means, electronic or mechanical, including photocopy, recording or any other information storage and retrieval system, without prior permission in writing from the publisher.

Printed and bound in Singapore

LIVING IN
MAURITIUS
Traditional Architecture of Mauritius

Preface
Geneviève Dormann

Photographs
Christian Vaisse

Introduction
Christian Saglio

Text and captions
Isabelle Desvaux de Marigny & Henriette Valentin Lagesse
with the collaboration of
Jean-François Kœnig

Watercolours
Monique de la Vallée Poussin

LES EDITIONS DU PACIFIQUE

CONTENTS

ON THE VERANDAH 13
THE FATE OF THE DODO? 19
POPULAR DWELLINGS 41
PLANTATION HOUSES 53
PLATEAU HOUSES 75
URBAN ARCHITECTURE 119
'CAMPEMENTS' AND HOTELS 161
ARCHITECTURAL NOTEBOOK 177
'GONE WITH THE WIND' 199

MAP 204
GLOSSARY 205
BIBLIOGRAPHY 206
ACKNOWLEDGEMENTS 208

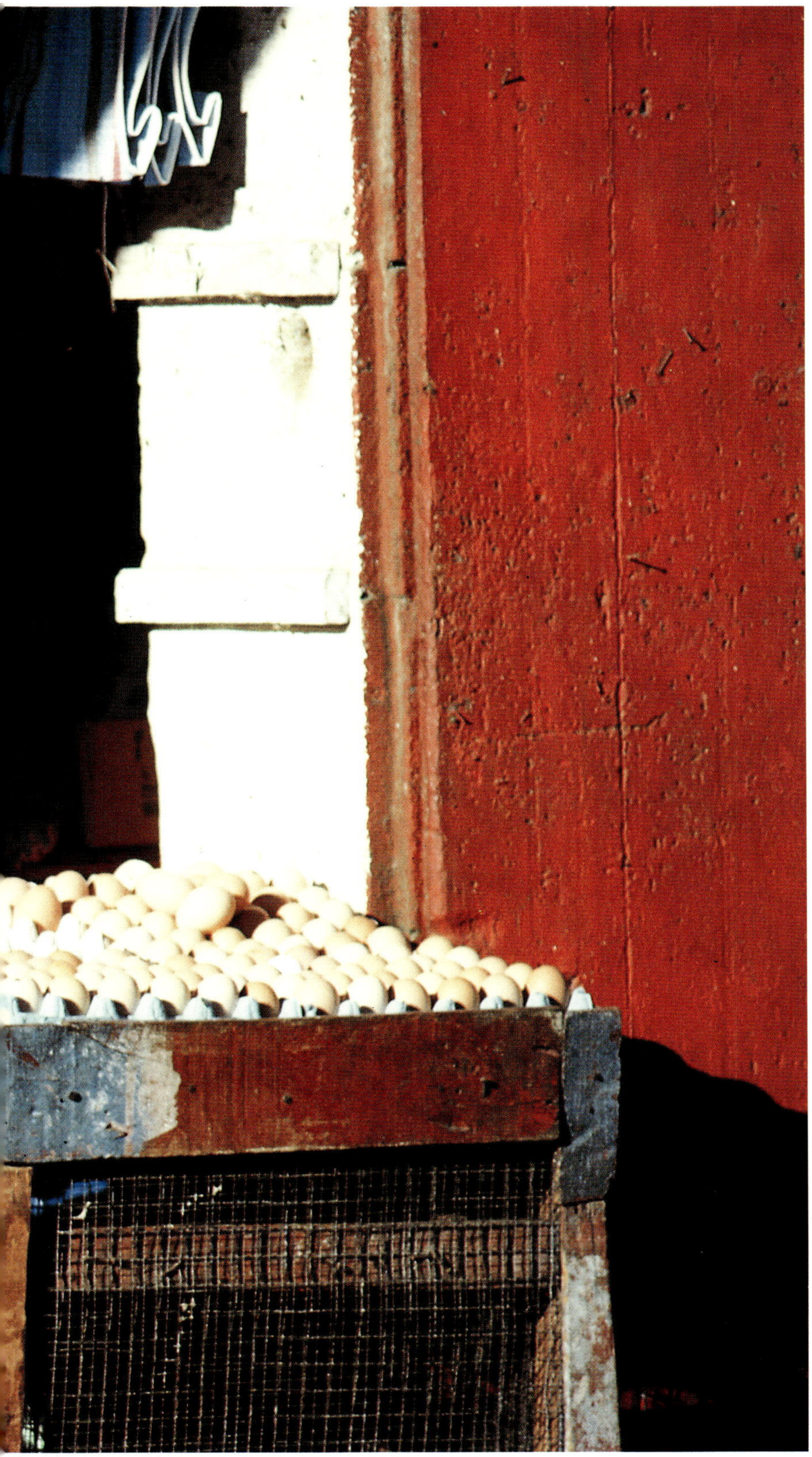

Eagle Brand
POUDRE A CARRI
Pour POISSON PIMENT
POUDRE A CARRI
Pour VIANDE Avec PIMENT
Ibrahim GOLAUP & CO. LTD
GRINDING MILL
14 MAMELON VERT STREET
Cotomill en poudre
IBRAHIMGOLAUP & CO
GRINDING MILL
PORT-LOUIS
SAFRAN
En Poudre
GRINDING MILL
14 MAMELON VERT STREET
PORT LOUIS
MADE IN MAURITIUS
80G
MOUTARDE 100%
EN POUDRE
Petit
TRADE

SENÉ
METI
MAMOURA
GROS HARÉ
PACK
PIPAR MOONG
SEL GLOBER
TOOKMARRIA.
Du Riz Plate
AJWAIN
PETIT HARÉ
PETIT ANIS
MANGRELLA
SEL EPSON
GINGELEE
BADAME
ANIS ETOILÉ
GIROFFE

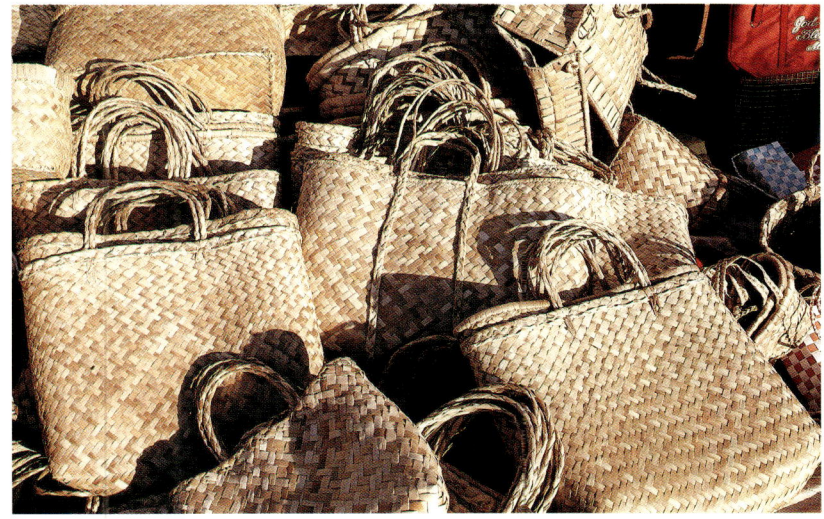

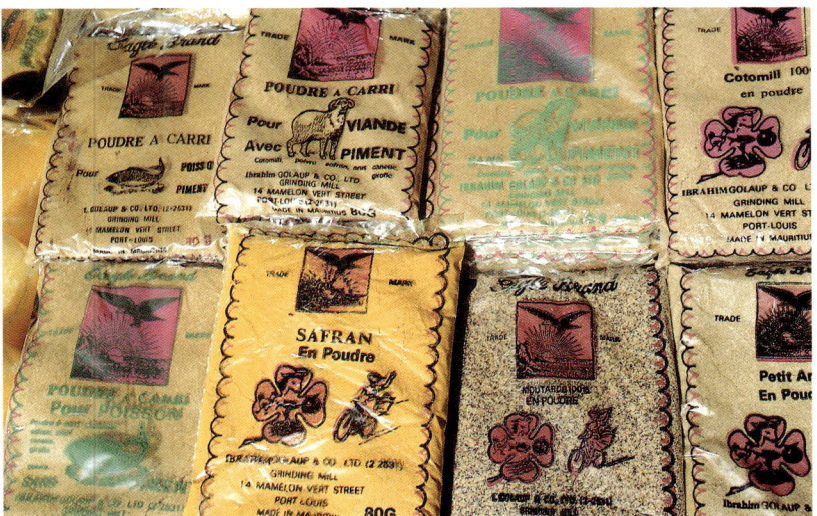

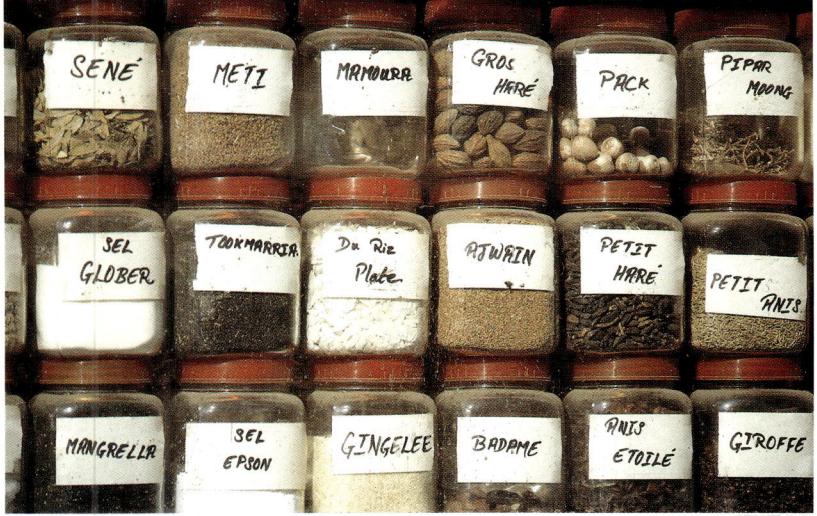

ON THE VERANDAH

Look carefully at the pictures in this superb album. They are precious because they pay tribute to the houses of Mauritius which we, perhaps, may be the last to know if the government of this country does not take the precautions necessary to preserve its heritage. Most of these houses are now more than a hundred years old; they tell of the efforts of a people to live harmoniously, struggling against the dangers of the sea, against the winds and the rain, and against time.

Their design, colours and fine decoration are inspired by the Orient, Africa and the Western world, creating a poetry that is far more moving than the photographs of Mauritius currently used by the advertising industry to promote package holidays. Within the pages of this book you will not find pictures of palm-fringed beaches or fluorescent swimming pools incarcerated in those concrete, air-conditioned hotels that are inevitably the same, from the Caribbean to the Bahamas, from the African coast to the holiday paradises of the Far East.

The human being features little amongst these pages, and yet they trace the story of two centuries of ingenuity and imagination, combining the basics for human survival with everyday comfort and poetry.

The book is also a cry for help, the second to my knowledge, appearing twelve years after Jean Louis Pagès' book, *Maisons Traditionelles de l'Ile Maurice* (Editions de l'Océan Indien). His illustrations aimed to champion the cause of the beautiful Mauritian houses — both patrician and popular — whose enormous charm

attracts the admiration of travellers from around the world. Indeed, with the vast tourism market now available to holiday-makers, the day of the single-minded sun-worshipper is passing. More and more, tourists want to discover the character and the soul, that is the history, of the country they visit. The remains of their heritage.

They prefer to stay in typical houses rather than hotels that are of an identical mould from one end of the planet to the other. Architects in Mauritius have just begun to realise this and are now beginning to build hotels which feature Creole-style bungalows.

Virtually every year a cyclone passes through the island, destroying vegetation and houses, only for the houses to be replaced by terrible concrete. Blocks dumped on the same spot, under a flat slab in guise of a roof, their walls punctuated by coffin-like windows, with thick grills to deter supposed burglars. Thus the concrete epidemic which raged in the sixties has ravaged parts of Mauritius, razing many beautiful houses that were still habitable, to replace them by sad constructions considered to be practical and rational by urban planners with no sense of aesthetics. At Port-Louis, the remains of beautiful eighteenth-century French architecture are being demolished to make way for buildings that are more profitable given the price of land in the middle of the town. At this very moment a group of Mauritian architects are begging the government to spare two ancient monuments on the Place des Armes; one of them, now the home of the national mint, was the bakery that sold biscuits and bread to the trading fleets on their way to the West Indies at the time of Labourdonnais.

This haste to destroy also derives — whether consciously or not — from a will to suppress all traces of European presence in Mauritius. The beautiful "colonial style" houses are actually the last vestiges of Creole architecture, based on two centuries of experience of living in the tropics. These houses, the beautiful houses pictured in this book, are at the risk of becoming, in our lifetime, mere memories.

Arguments to replace them with concrete are not convincing. It is obvious that wood is more fragile and requires more upkeep. Yet these well-loved old houses have nonetheless resisted, the majority of them for more than a century, the ravages of cyclones. Their sloping roofs keep out the heaviest rain and create a protective cushion of air above the living quarters, whereas the concrete roofs-cum-terraces are not totally watertight and are subject to an unfavourable thermal inertia: they retain the heat of the day and emit it during the night; patches of damp appear. The centre of Curepipe is thus disgraced by hideous blocks whose sides are streaked with long green water stains.

Over two centuries, the Mauritians have learned to build their houses to cope with the winds and the rain, the heat and the light. The first cases of Port-Louis were simple wooden boxes, roughly hewn and without foundations; they were often moved, in pieces or as a whole on rollers. Oiled paper served as glass for the windows. Shelter was not guaranteed: water would pour in when the rain was heavy. Under Mahé de Bourdonnais stone began to feature and some homes took on, in his memory, a Breton aspect. The beautiful Robillard family home at Mahébourg, now a museum, could easily have been built at Saint Malo or Saint-Servant.

Only later, with the arrival of the English, did comfort become a consideration. But wood remained the favoured material of the boatbuilders who were also responsible for building the first houses during the years of French rule on Mauritius.

There is a seaside "campement" on the west coast with walls of ravenala, a palm also known as "arbre du voyageur". These walls, made of layers of leaves, seem to be light and fragile. Yet the house stands up to cyclones for the simple reason that the the winds, instead of hitting it, go through it without harm. It is an effective symbol. Perhaps the same goes for life, and it is better to let yourself be buffeted by bad squalls than to oppose them with a rigid and inflexible mind. The first inhabitants of the island left traces of their vocabulary both in its architecture and its language. So we have the word "varangue" to describe the most important and the most appealing place in the Mauritian house. This word, that slips so easily off the tongue...is it a corruption of "veranda"? I prefer to associate it with the French word "varangue", denoting the piece of wood that protects the hull of a ship.

The verandah, place of passage and repose, surrounding or extending the house, is both sitting room and garden, an intermediary space between interior and exterior. It is a filter between the intimacy of the family sanctuary and the

unknown of the outside world. It is on the verandah that people receive a visitor and get to know him before allowing him to perpetrate to the heart of the home. It is a place of delicacy, of welcome but also of precaution. An invisible portcullis separates the verandah from the rest of the house.

For the people who live there, it is also an observation post. A true sailor is always looking out of the window of his house, either to check his boat at its mooring, or to watch out for invasion by the enemy. Even if he has no boat to tend, even if the enemy is not likely to appear over the horizon, the Mauritian islander always has a wandering eye, and the verandah is his domain. Hence the relatively large number of people who claim to have seen the celebrated green light, just before sunset. The green light is a product of the verandah. It is a place for the curious, where noises outside and movements of the neighbours can be heard. Nothing escapes the verandah where, in the shade of ferns and allamandas,

through the chinks of lowered blinds, the observer can see everything without being seen. Shaded against the sun, the heat of midday becomes bearable, while the little geckos, the good fairies of the verandah, fasten the suction pads of their feet to the walls and, with beating heart, swallow flies and mosquitoes with a well-aimed flick of the tongue. It is a place for relaxation where, even on the most sultry days, a light breeze skips across polished floors, an invisible fan to soothe burning foreheads.

The verandah is a place for dreams and gossip. The confidences of the verandah, always whispered, are tinted with the pastel shades of dawn, the gold of sunsets.

> *Aux pays du sucre et des mangues*
> *Les pales dames créoles*
> *S'éventent sous les farangues*
> *Au pays du sucre et des mangues*
> *Et zézaient de lentes paroles.*
> *(In the land of sugar and mangoes*
> *The pale Creole ladies*
> *Fan themselves under the verandahs*
> *In the land of sugar and mangoes*
> *And slowly lisp their words.)*
> Paul Jean Toulet, *Vers Inédits* (Bouquins Robert Laffont)

To live on the verandah is to choose to preserve, amidst our violent and nervous world, an interlude of grace and serenity. It is everything that we love.

Geneviève Dormann

THE FATE OF THE DODO?

Cap Malheureux, Crève-Coeur, Solitude, Baie du Tombeau, Pétrin, Grande Retraite, Fond du Sac...Land in Mauritius and plunge into its atmosphere of nostalgia, letting the names of towns and houses run through your mind and evoke their images according to the mood of the moment: Espérance, L'Aventure, Cachette, Providence, Trou aux Biches, Sans Souci, Poudre d'Or, Trou d'Eau Douce, Mon Repos, Bois d'Amourettes, Flic en Flac, Trou Fanfaron, Coin de Mire, Bel Ombre, Tour de l'Harmonie, Beaux Songes, Mon Désert-Mon Trésor...

The map of Mauritius reads like a poem, at times joyful, at times melancholy. I remember, as a child, that President Senghor once gave me a copy and I hung it on my bedroom wall where it remained long after. It was a constant reminder of how the president used it to illustrate his theories, declaring solemnly, "the Future and the Centre of the Universe are here!" He was no doubt alluding to the famous cultural and biological mixture produced by the charming melting pot that is Mauritius. This promised land has received the seeds of an incongruous multitude of races, religions and lifestyles from all the corners of the

Left: The statue of Mahé de Labourdonnais presides over the Place du Quai, Port-Louis.
Above: The old central market in Curepipe was built in 1917 by M Maurice Loumeau. It was destroyed in 1976.

earth. There might even be scope here for the in-vitro fertilisation of a "Universal Civilisation". Having immersed myself in this extraordinary maelstrom for a period of three years, I tend to agree with the president-cum-poet — who is also a member of the Académie Française.

But that is another story. My aim here is not to discuss the future of the Mauritian cultural kaleidoscope but to examine one of its most distinctive ingredients: the houses.

PLANET OF THE LITTLE PRINCE

On this "planet of the Little Prince, where all your dreams may come true"*, the houses are a part of the mirage. Each is unique and yet part of a harmonious whole. From the impressive residences of Curepipe to the small shops of Port-Louis, they combine a variety of influences, bearing witness to the panache and fantasy of a complex way of life that combines eighteenth century Versailles, British cosiness, African rhythm and Oriental mystery. Houses have been conceived to adapt to the ever-changing climate of an island where technicoloured rainbows divide the sky and where, at any time of day, and at any place or altitude, the traveller can pass in less than half an hour from a real London fog to the blue sea and blazing sun of the tourist brochures.

The *varangue* or verandah is the only defence against these charming inconsistencies. An intrinsic, and almost metaphysical, part of the Mauritian soul, the verandah plays the many roles of entrance, hall, terrace, tearoom, deck and conservatory. The verandah has a whole way of life of its own: the play of light and shade determined by the raising and lowering of raffia blinds which are painted the same colour as the shingled roof. The very word "varangue" becomes as essential to the foreign traveller as it is to the old native. A house in the garden and a garden in the house... this is what

*Antoine de St-Exupéry, *Le Petit Prince*, Hachette, 1945.

The verandah at Le Réduit is festooned with tropical greenery.

Mr Henri Harel's house in Curepipe, next to the Town Hall. It was demolished in the fifties (photo 1927).

verandah living is all about. It is a century-old way of life that continues still: I will always cherish dearly the memory of those dear old ladies who welcomed me on the *varangue* of their large wooden homes.

Mauritian houses are evocative of ships... Built by naval carpenters, they retained the spirit, appearance and framework of a ship and they seem ready to set sail at any moment. Baudelaire, whose famous poem *A une dame créole* was inspired by Mauritius, maintained that "décrire c'est dégrader et se dégrader"*. I will therefore avoid writing a descriptive inventory which takes account of the least important door handle. The photographs that follow are sufficiently eloquent. It can only be hoped that the superb images contained in this book will not become the sole remaining testimony to an architecture submerged by a tide of concrete.

THE PROMISED LAND

Mauritius has its origins in every corner of the globe. On arrival, the traveller's first impression is one of recognition rather than discovery, a feeling which probably stems from the global ancestry of the island. After solving the riddles of the map (strangely reminiscent of childhood treasure hunts), I immediately recognised the familiar faces of the mountains transformed into human beings by Malcolm de Chazal, the surrealist author (according to whom, "On Mauritius, we cultivate sugar cane and preconceptions"); the gentle and chaste waterfalls of *Paul et Virginie;* the pirates and buccaneers of *Treasure Island;* the deserted coves haunted by Robinson Crusoe; the blue lagoons of picture postcards; and the houses straight out of *Gone with the Wind....* all those places I had

*"To describe is to degrade and to degrade oneself."

The Hôtel de Ville of Curepipe with, in the foreground, the well-loved statue of Paul and Virginie.

long cherished in my imagination before I finally came across them in reality.

Behind the stereotypes — landscapes created for the setting for a popular musical or to be reproduced on holiday postcards — are traces of days gone by. One can still feel the strange and powerful fascination of forgotten worlds, man being, after all, but a brief incident in the history of this very old piece of land. Millions of years had elapsed before the arrival, only a few centuries ago, of the first navigators, the Arabs, the Portuguese and the Dutch. The explorers were followed by corsairs and gentlemen farmers from Brittany, the younger sons of titled families who came in the hope of finding fame and fortune in the tropics. Then it was the turn of the bands of suffering slaves uprooted from Africa or Madagascar. Only in 1810 (after the British landing at Cap Malheureux) did British soldiers and civil servants — dilettantes and fair-play denizens — begin to settle. Thereafter came successive waves of immigrants, mostly tradesmen and agricultural workers from China and the Indian sub-continent.

During the first three hundred years of settlement in this promised land, man had managed to preserve a balance with nature. The absence of humanity for so long can still be felt strongly in many parts of the island. But recently it would seem that the human machine has lost control and that the traditional Mauritian houses are to be its first victims.

Above left: Tea at Britannia Savanne. From left: T W Innes, J G Gibson, A Mac Millan, Mrs Innes.
Above right: The sitting room at Chateaufort (photo 1932).

Ephemeral, Alas...

I have always admired the grace of things ephemeral — except in the case of houses. When he is wandering in foreign parts, the traveller depends on his ports of call. Fortunately for him, houses must remain where they are. In his nomadic existence of comings and goings, voyages, encounters, departures, rediscoveries and more or less final goodbyes, houses are the only constant landmarks and retreats.

The wooden houses of Mauritius are, by nature, ephemeral. Here, more than elsewhere, "les maisons sont fugitives, hélas, comme les années..."* (Baudelaire). Precariously poised between past and present, they need to be loved to survive the ravages of cyclones, termites and, above all, property developers.

Atmosphere, Atmosphere

"Objets inanimés, auriez-vous donc une âme?..."**(Baudelaire) These old wooden houses throb and breathe and warp and shrink; in short, they live. Modern houses are rarely capable of inspiring dreams.

Why this passion for the Mauritian "painted ladies" (a term of endearment often applied to San Francisco's wooden houses), this dogged determination not to compromise when they are threatened? Why this irresistible urge to cross their threshold, to discover their secrets, to invade and conquer them? Why this need to understand them and to be adopted by them? Perhaps because there emanates from them a disquieting atmosphere, redolent of both sensuality and spirituality, a charm that captures the imagination and the soul.

Their reputation of being haunted comes from their touching combination of strength and vulnerability. They appear suddenly round the corner of a drive, their blue-shingled roofs

*"Houses, alas, are as fleeting as time itself..."
**"Lifeless objects, might there yet be a soul in you?" (Baudelaire)

Above centre: Destruction at Montalieu, Curepipe, following cyclone Carol (photo 1960).
Above right: View of a house at the foot of Moka hill (engraving by Milbert).

set against a backdrop of sky and mountains, like wafting, insubstantial ghosts but always rooted in the most perfect location. These houses are the stuff of which our dreams are made: we recognise them at once. But we must learn to keep peace with them, to respect them and to listen to them before they exclude us from their secrets forever.

It is difficult to determine exactly why one is

moved by certain places and certain people. Perhaps it is due to those minute peculiarities which reflect their deeper nature, or because of some mysterious affinity which creates the magic of a meeting. One has only to isolate the components of charm in order to become immune to it. Yet, although I have studied and

Above right: The entrance hall at Mongoust (reconstruction by Jean Lejuge de Segrais).

examined them for a long time, the houses of Mauritius continue to seduce me. I almost share the common belief that they are haunted. Within these houses I have often sensed more mystery and esoteric animism than in the depths of the sacred forests of Africa.

The old wooden houses are never completely silent. Each one has its own orchestration of sounds. They may reassure you or disturb you but they always keep you company. Creaks, whispers, hushes, gasps, squeaks, footsteps...a multitude of signs and signals enliven the solemn silence of these houses "where footsteps have a meaning..." (Baudelaire).

BRIEF ENCOUNTERS

I feel that I have met some of these houses in the same way that one meets people; they have just as much to tell. Houses permeated my life in Mauritius and dwelt in me just as I dwelt in them.

It is hard to describe these encounters: memories flood through my mind pell-mell after umpteen moves from house to house. I changed house ten times in three years and, whether big or small, I loved each house in a different way.

Château la Misère at Cap Malheureux; the

Above left: The former convent of the Sisters of Lorette in Port-Louis nestles at the foot of the citadel.
Above right: Mongoust in the days of its glory (photo 1883).

Résidence Bagatelle at Mon Désert-Mon Trésor; Villa Mon Désir at Flic en Flac; Maison Mon Goût at Grande Retraite; the islands: Pourquoi Pas?; Mouchoir Rouge; Deux Cocos. I devised a game with these addresses and could not resist writing them in turn (except for the islands and Flic en Flac) on my Parisian cheques. I enjoyed the consternation of petrol attendants on French motorways who would ask without fail: "Are you sure this can be cashed in France?"

La Malmaison

In 1903, La Malmaison was moved from Moka to Curepipe to be used as the Town Hall. This was in the days when houses were often displaced with the purchase of a new property or as the result of a marriage or an epidemic.

La Malmaison was my first encounter with a Mauritian house and, in many ways, it remains the most spectacular. I came across it on a typically gloomy and wet Curepipe afternoon, the day after my arrival in Mauritius, when it appeared like a ghost out of the drizzly mist so suggestive of Brittany...an abandoned wreck, its limbs still quivering...as if in the final throes of death.

Reality only affects us when it begins to embody our fantasies, when our imagination is captured by certainty. "Do these fairy-tale houses really exist?...", I asked myself. Facing this queen of Mauritian houses, I was reminded of all the castles of my childhood dreams, of *Gone with the Wind* and *Sleeping Beauty*. "Home, home...", like ET, I was back home at last. I responded to the call of the house.

On my first day I had fallen for this queen, tattered but still resplendent with dignity and elegance. Surrounded by building sites, a bus stop, a nightmarish Hotel Europa, a casino, a stupefying covered market (originally destined to be an aquarium in Belgium, if Curepipian gossip is to be believed), La Malmaison has managed to preserve her forsaken majesty.

The fervent advocates of concrete were apparently disappointed that the last cyclones did not succeed in "doing away once and for all with the problematic Town Hall." They had plans for a wonderful five-storey building to take its place. But La Malmaison has survived worse threats and is now awaiting renovation.

La Rocherie

The Maison Carné, donated to the church by the Comtesse de Carné, was my second encounter. I entered it as one does a sanctuary, just before the heirs sold off to the highest bidder the furniture and every trace of the old Comtesse (who died at the age of 103!). It was an almost sacrilegious stripping down during which all the contents of the house, including photograph albums, mirrored wardrobes, curtain rails and large enamelled baths with griffins' feet, were dispersed, along with all the memories and the very atmosphere of the place. Immediately before the kill, everything

was in its place, just as in the good old days, and I could not resist the temptation of pushing the ivory button of the mahogany bellpull that was hanging over the bed. The bell still rang in the pantry, like a voice from the past.

Eureka

"It is to this house, the most important place for my family, that I must now return... A mythical house to me as I only ever heard of it in terms of a lost house... White, light, standing against a range of mountains whose names seemed magical to me: Le Pouce, les Deux Mamelles, le Pieter Both... No other house will ever be so important, no other will ever possess such a soul...vast and silent amidst the secret solitude of its earthly paradise, retaining in its heart the remembrance of its birth, like a place to which one never returns?" (J.M.G. Le Clézio, *Voyages à Rodrigues*, Journal Gallimard, 1985)

Euréka has been saved from demolition. "The great wooden house with its hundred French windows" has been turned into a museum. You can have lunch there on the large verandah and listen to your host recount endless anecdotes about the Le Clézio family.

The lengthy and extravagant saga is rather like "Dallas in Moka". Euréka's history is composed of a Balzacian world with eccentric, all-powerful great-aunts, disputes over acres of sugar cane, divisions of factories, squandered rupees, solicitors and legacies.

POURQUOI PAS?

An island within the island of Mauritius, Pourquoi Pas? is an island-house that floats capriciously (why not?...) in the middle of the Roches Noires lagoon. I had often sailed around it before finally landing and spending some time there.

It is a sunny weekend refuge from the mists of the upper plateau. I loved its makeshift and casual appearance, defying the sedate concrete of the seaside *campements*. (The term "campement" originally referred to a weekend house made of ravenala and straw. Whole families — and most of their belongings — used to move from the upper plateau to "go camping" in the summer months. Nowadays, the word is applied to the ever-multiplying concrete villas that house the tourists.) I also loved its frayed filaos, its tall verandah patched up after each cyclone and its half-hidden approach via a wobbly old pontoon stretched over the turquoise lagoon. On Pourquoi Pas?, one has only to turn one's head to watch the setting of the sun and the rising of the moon on the same evening: a rare privilege in Mauritius.

Not far from here is the St Geran channel, the site of the famous shipwreck that was immortalised in Bernadin de St Pierre's novel *Paul et Virginie*. Virginie, draped in her virginity, dies at the prow of the sinking ship amid the foaming waves, a tragic victim of her modesty. This is more than the melodramatic, flowery and exotic novelette that some censors would have us believe. To be carried away into an almost

Above centre: The statue of Paul and Virginie at Curepipe.
Above left: Maison Blanche.

biblical paradise by its chaste eroticism, the reader should turn its pages on this very stretch of water, between the islands of Pourquoi Pas? and Ambre.

Villa Cayeux

"Diplomat looking for large wooden house..." This small advertisement went against the trend of all the others which abound in the Mauritian daily newspapers: "Prestigious concrete villa to let"..."To sell: excellent wood from demolished property". My advertisement was deliberately provocative in the context of an era when many beautiful houses were condemned or moribund, awaiting the fate of those which had already disappeared. It led to some memorable encounters with houses and their owners, who have since become my friends.

As soon as I set foot upon its creaking floorboards, I fell in love with the Villa Cayeux and began to try to comprehend it. Our idyll lasted for a year. The house was elegant and melancholy, with its ornate wrought-iron balustrade, its colonnaded verandah and its sky-blue roof (of that nondescript and sublime blue that is particular only to Curepipe when, for once, it does not rain). The same pastel shades prevailed in the garden: the mauves, blues, pinks and whites of hydrangeas, begonias, camelias, orchids, azaleas and lily of the valley. Inside, the pastel world continued. This house was my refuge: I felt completely at home amidst its faded wallpapers, its crystal chandeliers, its four-poster beds, its mirrored wardrobes, its ever-extendable dining table, its easy chairs, sideboards, sofas, pedestal tables, consoles, upholstered armchairs and writing desks... There was a whole series of large dimly-lit rooms with creaking floorboards and communicating doors whose handles were made of brass or crystal. One of these doors led to an incongruous early-thirties bathroom with shiny green ceramic tiles which looked almost

Above: Villa Cayeux has been dismantled to be rebuilt on the island of Deux Cocos.

good enough to eat!

In this house prowled a rather distant and austere presence, known by visiting friends as "the ghost". We built up an excellent working relationship that was both considerate and demanding. He knew how to test us and manifested himself through a profusion of sounds and an avalanche of coded messages. I would fall asleep to the muffled sound of rain streaming down the roof and would be awakened by silence. I would lie listening to the house...was someone walking in the attic, or breathing behind the door, or was the ghost simply disappearing into the bedroom wardrobe? A haunted house generally mirrors one's own dreams...

After the death of its owner, the Villa Cayeux was to be demolished and replaced by soulless — and ghostless — blocks of flats. It was saved by an unbelievable stroke of luck and has been dismantled with great care, plank by plank, to be rebuilt on the island of Deux Cocos, where it will have a new lease on life. (This used to be a fairly regular occurrence in Mauritius. Houses would be moved as new properties were acquired, when people were married or when epidemics threatened. Nowadays, houses are rarely displaced, the last case being the Curepipe Town Hall — in 1903.) As for the Villa Cayeux, I wish it as happy a transplantation as as that of the Scottish ghost in René Clair's film *Ghost for Sale*. Deported to California, it wandered as a lost soul until (the typically happy Hollywood ending) its reincarnation and marriage to a rich heiress.

PELL-MELL

It is impossible to describe all my encounters; each Mauritian house has its own personality and atmosphere, its stories and anecdotes. Although they are not invulnerable, they are inexhaustible story-tellers.

I will conclude pell-mell with a medley of impressions: Château Guimbeau at the entrance to Curepipe, like a reward after the slow crawl from Plaisance* airport, sandwiched between smoky buses and rows of concrete structures promoting Pepsi and Coca Cola; the small

---

*"Plaisance" was an auspicious name for an airport, but, like the Pamplemousses Gardens, it has been renamed Sir Seewoosagur Ramgoolam Airport, in memory of the Father of Independence.

fisherman's house on the island of Mouchoir Rouge adrift on Mahébourg, the loveliest lagoon of Mauritius; the rectory of the Immaculate Conception in Port-Louis where Père Souchon invited me to discover the marvellous attic and where I first fell in love with the indefinable grey-green Wedgwood blue which has since become my favourite colour; Sorèze House whose colonnades are hidden behind a romantic copse; the Hôtel International, last refuge of Malcolm de Chazal, with its antique ceiling fans and its map of France dating from the fifties; the Point de Vénus, beaten by the trade winds, atop a hill on the small island of Rodrigues (600 kilometres east of Mauritius), basking in the old world atmosphere of a kind of Irish Africa where polkas, waltzes and quadrilles are still the order of the day at village fairs; la Sablonnière, now the "Le Gourmet" restaurant (arrive there in the evening, preferably under a tropical

downpour so that the maître d'hôtel will come out with an umbrella to meet you at the foot of the steps, before you dine looking out over an Eiffel Tower (built in 1889) that rises — like a hallucination — from between two palm trees; the island of Deux Cocos and its turn-of-the-century folly, a neo-Moorish patio of pink, rough-cut colonnades and arcades set on the white sands of Blue Bay; La Tour Blanche, looming over the waterfalls of the valley of Beau-Bassin whence, so the legend goes, Darwin set off astride an elephant (imported from India) on his search to prove his theory of evolution; Villa Wiehe in Floréal, the most

Above: The verandah at Chateaufort exudes elegance and dignity.
Above right: Constructed in 1870, the Royal Alfred Observatory was abandoned in 1959 and demolished soon after.

reserved and charming of all the Mauritian homes I discovered, like a face whose features are not immediately striking, but whose impression grows on you and never leaves you... So many houses, so many encounters, so many anecdotes...

The following houses are but a more few that cannot be omitted from my lengthy honours list: Château Trompette with its long drive and turrets, Béthanie with its "escarpolette", *varangue* and fountain, and, last but not least, the large Moolan residence on the Champ de

Above: "Some Mauritian houses" from A Mac Millan's Mauritius Illustrated *(London, 1914).*

Mars, Bel Air, Surprise, Saint Antoine, Esperanza, Belle Vue, Le Mesnil, Mauricia, the Harel houses in Curepipe, Riche en Eau, Le Coconut, La Villebague, Champrosay, Labourdonnais, Mon Rêve, Beau Séjour, the Monte Carlo guest house, Poncini, Verdun, La Tour Koenig, Bel Ombre, L'Arbre Rouge, the Geber House, the naval museum at Mahébourg and all those houses that still hold out against the concrete invasion that is threatening Vacoas, Curepipe, Quatre Bornes, Phoenix or Rose Hill. I must also commend the Plaza Theatre (1934) and the theatre at Port-Louis where strange echoes are created by the wooden auditoriums.

In Port-Louis every façade tells its story. Remnants of successive civilisations that have invaded and left their mark are easily recognisible: the British racecourse; eighteenth-century French squares; Oriental boutiques, African markets and Chinese casinos; temples, mosques and cathedrals; winding lanes and wide avenues lined with palm trees; wrought-iron balconies, their windows and shutters open or shut according to the breeze, heat, light or desire for privacy of the occupants... Port-Louis is an old city made up of this and that, a place where it is pleasant to stroll in the cool of the evening when the crowds of commuters have left for home.

The Fate of the Dodo

Little time remains, however. Port-Louis is surrendering its character to an advancing army of bulldozers and concrete mixers. As Levi-Strauss said, "Mankind is creating a mass civilisation, it is settling down into a monoculture": even in this remote land of sugar cane the march towards uniformity is already taking its toll. Gone with the wind are our childhood fantasies

Above: The central railway station, Port-Louis (photo 1901).

and dreams. "Brick upon brick I'll get my block," rings an African nursery rhyme, a refrain that often comes to haunt my mind.

Mauritius is burying her soul in a concrete vault. Anyone can build anything — anywhere. The magic of this little island, this fairyland where Malcolm de Chazal breathed life into the mountains, is fading and giving way to stereotyped tower blocks typical of any European suburb. As Mauritius is developed, it slowly loses its identity: that special *je ne sais quoi*, those elusive elements that composed its charm. Lagoons, mountains, forests, sugar cane fields and wooden houses are being eaten up by apartment blocks, by factories and by land division. Is it really necessary for progress to eliminate systematically the history, variety and individuality of a country?

Singapore's remedy (late but effective) has proved that it is possible to reconcile development with architectural heritage and that the past does offer assets for the future. "Architecture should read like a book": there is no need to tear out the first pages in order to write the following ones. Recent achievements by some Mauritian architects have shown that, after all, it is possible to incorporate old and new into a harmonious blend.

The government, for its part, has begun to realise that it might be detrimental to pile up storey upon storey — like noughts upon a balance sheet. It recently vetoed the construction of a skyscraper in Port-Louis which would have razed to the ground an eighteenth century building on the famous Place d'Armes.

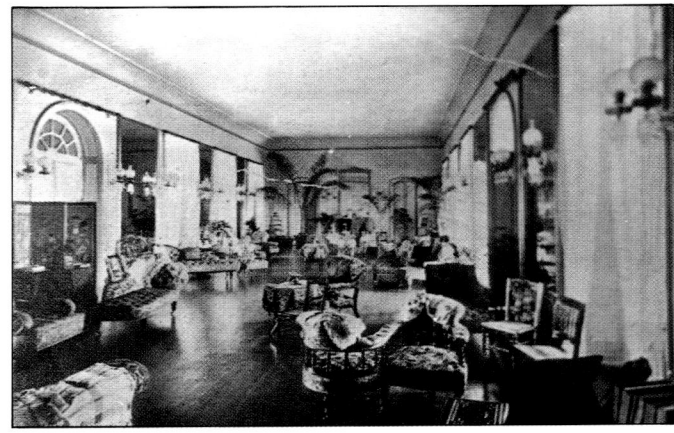

Perhaps the wooden houses of Mauritius will escape the fate of the dodo (*Didus ineptus*), that large turkey-like bird with atrophied wings whose survival (until the arrival of the Dutch in 1598) exemplified Darwin's theories, but whose disappearance and posthumous fame now only provide copy for tourist brochures. Yet, in the words of Malcolm de Chazal, "To resign oneself is to consign hope to the deep-freeze."

Christian Saglio

The interior of Le Réduit betrays the comfortable existence of its owners.

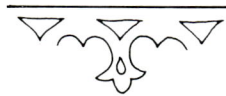

A typical house in Curepipe displays many traditional architectural features (photo 1953).

POPULAR DWELLINGS

The creativity and inspiration behind these houses is equalled only by their apparent joie-de-vivre. Flaunting the conventions of traditional architecture, their riotous colours and abundant decoration are a feast for the eyes. The care with which they were built is a reflection of the pride of the multi-cultural community of Mauritius in their homes: Mauritian style is not difficult to achieve assuming one is willing simply to try.

Up until the 1930s the majority of agricultural and factory workers lived in *cases* as primitive as those of the settlers of the eighteenth century. Most of their houses were built of uncut stone or wattle-and-daub covered with a straw roof. Corrugated iron and brightly-coloured paint — features which now characterise the popular dwelling — date from the 1930s when an increased number of agricultural workers became land owners.

The houses are an adaptation of the existing style of traditional architecture employed by all Mauritians, irrespective of their cultural background. The popular dwelling is a colourful, asymmetric version of the larger house to which a profusion of decoration has been added.

The kitchen is a small separate structure at the rear of the house, situated in a compound amongst the chicken coops, where the smoky smell of burning wood mingles with the sharp odour of spices crushed on the *roche carri*.

The pride with which the owner looks after his house can be detected in its neat and well-kept interior and its brilliantly polished red floor, known locally as a *châlis*. The walls are covered with a multitude of memorabilia but pride of place is always given to religious images.

In Mauritius even the small houses generally have an impressive garden for, climate permitting, Mauritians tend to live outside, or on the verandah, rather than in the house. However tiny, the garden is as picturesque as the house. Unlike their dignified formal counterparts on the plateau or the plantation, these gardens are a jumble of flowers and fruit trees, vegetables and medicinal herbs, a taste of the infinite colour and variety of tropical flora.

Page 36: *House on the sugar plantation of St Aubin.*

Pages 38-39: *The casuarina tree, commonly known as "filaos", lends the costline of Maurius its particular identity, often a surprise for the visitor who expects the standard palm groves. The casuarina was introduced by the Abbé Rochon who visited Mauritius in 1768.*

Page 40: *This house nestles amidst dense greenery at the foot of the mountains. One can almost feel the coolness of the air and hear the cock crow.*

Left: *Worn by the passage of time, this house is so in keeping with its surroundings that it appears to have grown out of the ground.*

Right: *These popular dwellings form an intrinsic part of the traditional architecture which gives Mauritius its character. It is to be hoped that they will become a source of inspiration for contemporary buildings.*

Although the architecture of his house follows a certain pattern of rules, every individual is his own architect. Each house is the expression of his creative spirit, although, generally a certain number of established rules are respected. The house is raised off the ground; its roof or roofs are sloping (and often made of corrugated iron); its gables are ventilated by a small slatted window; for the openings, there are two alternatives: either the doors and windows open directly onto the interior, protected by corrugated iron canopies and wooden shutters, or there is a verandah, enclosed by small-paned windows.

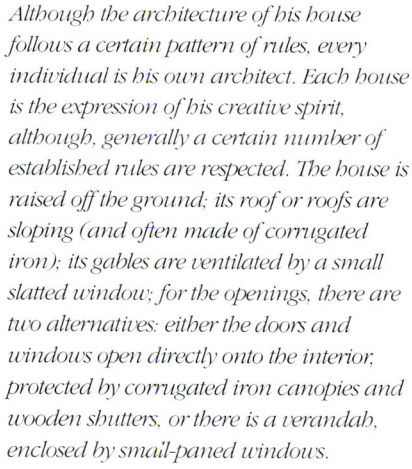

Above: *Owners whose houses look straight onto the street have devised ingenious ways of shielding themselves from the intrusive eyes of passers-by. In this house small wooden panels cover the lower part of the windows.*

Above right: *The style of these dwellings confirms that traditional architecture is not limited to the large wooden residences built by plantation owners.*

Right: *The glazed verandah, however modest, can be a source of inspiration for the revival of modern architecture. It is possible to manufacture on a large scale, reproducing traditional details and using metal instead of wood.*

Above: *Although popular dwellings are usually rural, there are many examples of colourful popular boutiques, such as this one in Floréal. Traditional architecture often features later additions that blend with elegance into the existing structure. Here the living quarters are more recent than the shop below.*

Left: *Simplicity in a verandah often betrays the fact that it is modern. This may be a matter of taste or it may be due to a lack of skilled craftsmen. With the encroaching tide of concrete in Mauritius it is true that many of the crafts traditionally passed from father to son have been lost. Nowadays, however, there is a glimmer of a revival of old-fashioned trades.*

Above: *Traditional architecture often displays a surprising simplicity and lack of decorative detail in its design.*
Right: *The popular dwelling is usually set in a well-kept garden, a reflection of the care and pride of the owner.*

Above: *A juxtapostion of startling colours produces a boldly patterned tableau of naïve art.*
Right: *The most touching dwellings are family houses whose simplicity lends richness.*

Above: *It would seem that an artist used all the tints and hues of his palate to compose this picture.*
Left: *Timber shingles are sometimes used to cover the walls of houses.*

Every facade is unique in its detail. The decorative trim of the verandah and the canopy, the contours of the window surrounds, and the finials are charming examples of local craftsmanship.

PLANTATION HOUSES

We are in nineteenth century Mauritius, silver cane flowers shimmering against a clear blue sky and the sweet smell of sugar hanging heavy in the air. A tall factory chimney billows clouds of smoke, and all around is a bustle of activity. Beyond, in an arbour of greenery, is the house, noble and majestic, the abode of the planter.

Times have changed but traditions remain. Today, Mauritius still lives to the rhythm of the sugar industry, and most of the houses that were built with the factories have been jealously preserved. The plantation manager generally enjoys the privilege of the house for the duration of his duties.

They can be seen all over the island, wherever sugar cane cultivation provoked the construction of factories. Unfortunately all that now remains of most factories is the large store chimney. Up until 1860 as many as two hundred and sixty plantations existed, but the grand plantation houses were found only on the larger plantations. As years went by plantations were annexed, and there are now only nineteen sugar factories in Mauritius.

It is difficult to define the style of the plantation house. Nowhere are the differences in appearance so marked whilst yet remaining within the traditional mould. There are houses with two storeys and houses with only one, houses with turrets and those with circular verandahs. But despite their many differences they are united by their size and their lack of elaborate detail.

The interiors are usually as grand and large in scale as the house itself. Spacious and airy reception rooms are opulently furnished with imposing sideboards, dining tables for twenty people or more, and elegant chairs and sofas.

The magnificent grounds with century-old trees and vast expanses of lawn add a further dimension to these sumptuous dwellings.

Page 53 and left: *La Villebague owes its name to the estate of La Villebague in St Méloir des Ondes, to the east of St Malo in Brittany. The plantation started producing sugar in 1743, one of the first to do so. The house was built around 1759 by the French governor René Magon who took as his model the Governor's Palace in Pondicherry. The turrets were added in 1934, completely changing the aspect of what was previously a manor house typical of eighteenth century France. Usually turrets feature only on houses with one storey, but La Villebague is an exception to the rule.*

Above: *The verandahs of large houses are often paved with stone.*

Right: *Strong sunlight projects a distorted image of a rattan sofa.*

Beau Sejour is situated at the end of a long avenue of royal palm trees, a surprisingly French approach to a house that was originally built by the British. Originally built by the Anglo-Ceylon Company around 1890, Beau Sejour was rebuilt in 1920, using concrete for the walls and joists. The use of timber for the roof and floors ensured that the charm of this large house was preserved.

Rays of sun transform this simple fountain at Beau Sejour into a shower of light. Overleaf: Bel Air St Felix was built in the second half of the nineteenth century by the great-grandfather of the present owner who acquired the sugar plantation in 1850. These photographs depict the two dimensions of life on the verandah: the area at the front, with its elegant cane furniture and pot plants, is the place where guests are entertained, and the family domain, within the privacy of the glazed verandah, is at the back. Doors open on each axis, allowing the gentle sea breeze to circulate through the house.

Left: *In the 1880s Mauricia belonged to an English gentleman whose favourite pastime was growing sweet-peas. Their exquisite aroma was a joy for all those who came to the property. The house was demolished by cyclone Carol in 1960 and subsequently rebuilt on the existing foundations, retaining its old world atmosphere.*
Above: *The formality of the gardens of Mauricia is accentuated by their surroundings — a sea of sugar cane fields on all four sides.*

Pages 62-63: *Built at Plaisance around 1870 this house was demolished and rebuilt at Riche-en-Eau in 1890. The new owner transformed it from a two-storey into a single-storey house and introduced the idea of double columns. The gardens reflect the French character of their creator Mr Rochecouste, with their formal lawns, large pools, well-kept alleyways and topiary. An old stone arch covered in greenery greets the visitor at the entrance.*

Far left: *This property was purchased by an Indian in 1898. Although he never came to Mauritius he sent emissaries to build the grand house known as Bel Ombre. It was designed by an architect who was also responsable for the construction of several public buildings in Port-Louis.*

Above and left: *Louvres and raffia blinds of Bel Ombre filter out the strength of the sun.*

Above: *This bell was salvaged from the wreck of the* Clan Campbell, *the first steam boat of the Clan line to come to Mauritius. It met its fate on the reef opposite Bel Ombre in September 1882.*

Left and right: *Much of the furniture of Bel Ombre was rescued from the Rouillard residence in Curepipe when it was demolished. Originally all of the glass in the doors was coloured.*

Left: *Labourdonnais remains one of the few houses built according to strictly-defined plans under the supervision of a French architect (M. Rampant). Work started in 1856 and was completed in 1858.*
Above: *The French windows of the pavilion, built in 1910.* "It was not uncommon here in this island for three or four sons or sons-in-law with their wives and families to live in their own pavilions on the old people's estate, meeting at breakfast and dinner around the family table." (Bengal Civilian, 1835)

"In that land of the sun, the purity of the atmosphere, the rich and magical lines of colour, the softness of the aerial perspective, the powerful relief of light and shadows produce impressions of pleasure rarely equalled even in our finest days..." (Frederic Mouat). Simple and majestic, this verandah derives its style from its imposing dimensions and from its harmony of form and tone. Before wickerwork became fashionable at the beginning of this century the furniture on the verandah was much the same as in the sitting room: armchairs, sofas and cane-bottomed chairs.

Above: This magnificent avenue of Chinese banyan trees (Ficus retusa) was planted around 1820. It is very likely that it led to the house that existed previously on the site of Labourdonnais.
Right: The wrought-iron balustrade of Labourdonnais is one of the finest on the island.

Above: *In this ancestral home every suite of furniture has its story; and every story is irrevocably entangled with the past. Rarely would a Mauritian home have displayed features as sophisticated as these: the tapestry, the chandelier, the panelled doors and the French parquet flooring are signs of the original occupants' close contacts with their homeland.*

Left: *In his* Rambles around Mauritius *of 1855, Mr Clark refers to the well-maintained kitchen garden and its delicious fruit and vegetables.*

The furniture in the dining room and the study was bought by Henry Barlow during on of his voyages to London in the 1850s. The tapestry, ordered in 1906 to replace the original one, was made in Alsace.
Overleaf: The Burke Hotel was built in 1840, a rustic structure, probably thatched, on the road to Forest Side. It was destroyed by a cyclone in 1872. The existing house, known as Les Aubineaux, was built by M. Bestel. Its numerous embellishments, notably the turrets, were added at a later date by the Rochecouste and the Guimbeau families.

PLATEAU HOUSES

Hidden hither and thither along the winding roads which criss-cross the upper plateau, these houses come in all shapes and sizes.

Towards the end of the nineteenth century, two simultaneous influences — a malaria epidemic and the expansion of the railways — encouraged the expansion of this region. The malaria epidemic was so devastating that many Mauritians moved from the low-lying Pamplemousses and Port-Louis area to the plateau where the climate was supposed to be more salubrious. For a long time, Moka was the place to be. Villas sprung up along the main road which hugs the mountain range. A few families have remained faithful to this area, but most moved to the Plaines Wilhems as more facilities became available in the towns on the central railway line. As the railways were extended, office workers began to commute to Port-Louis and so the trend to move was further encouraged.

French nineteenth-century architecture was traditionalist in comparison with the British taste for the picturesque: the charm of the plateau house lies in its combination of both these tendencies.

Its variety of silhouettes contrasts with the simple shape of the early nineteenth-century house. The purity of the earlier form was enriched by new elements — a multitude of roof shapes, turrets, glazed verandahs, bow-windows, auvents — all of which created endless imaginative possibilities.

Despite the variety of forms, one can distinguish four broad categories in this region: houses with simple large columns; those with a colonnade and balustrade; those with turrets; and those with glazed verandahs. Of course some houses belong to more than one category. Plateau houses basically being suburban dwellings, the size of the garden usually reflects the size of the house: large houses have large gardens; small houses have small gardens.

Far left: Eureka at Moka has been a museum since 1986 and is the only Mauritian house complete with period furniture that is open to the public. With its 14 rooms and 109 doors and windows, it is the largest house on the island. It was built in 1830 by Mr Carr, an eminent Scot who wanted to live in close proximity to the Governor's residence at La Réduit. From 1856 to 1986 it was the home of the Leclezio family.

Left: This cast-iron four-poster bed is a rare sight on the island of Mauritius.

Below: The bathroom houses a collection of period pieces: an old-fashioned shower, a hip-bath and a washstand with its pitcher and basin. Cut from a single block of marble and weighing over 500 kilograms the bath is unique. It originates from India and was ordered in the eighteenth century by Mr Chintamun Gujadhur, a distinguished gentleman of Indian origin. Above the bath is an example of a wood-fuelled water heater.

Champrosay was built by an Englishman around 1850. It was acquired by the avid collector Mr Lois Le Vieux in 1967. The verandah exudes a typical aura of relaxation and well-being.

The formal sitting room. When Champrosay was purchased this room was divided by a partition and the door on the right had been done away with. During restoration work the door was rediscovered in the cellar and was immediately reinstated. The chandelier and the gilded bronze clock were originally in Valory, a large residence in Moka. The central table is probably an early nineteenth century British piece, of a style known locally as "East India Company". The cabinet on the left is thought to be an authentic Boulle; it is interesting to note that Mr Le Vieux discovered an identical cabinet in the Wallace Collection in London.

The study. On the wall above the desk (another "East India Company" piece) hangs a hand-embroidered tapestry depicting Van Dyck and Rembrandt. It is the work of the young ladies boarding at Madame Benoit's academy in 1860. The bronze statue of the god Pan is by Coysevox and dates from 1769.

Left: *In a country where one lives in close proximity with nature, it is often impossible to draw the line between house and garden. Here the house seems to be an extension of its garden.*

Above and right: *Against a back-drop of blue sky the symmetrical composition of the house is a successful synthesis of turrets, glazed verandah, window overhangs, dormer windows and decorative detailing.*

The play of light and shade on the verandah creates a strange graphic composition. "These houses were conceived and constructed at a time when daring and invention were in direct proportion to man's imagination. They exalt the knowledge of the forest ranger, the logcutter, the master sawyer and the squarer, as well as the skill of artisans of various trades: the stone-hewer, the mason, the smelter, the smith, the cabinet-maker, the joiner, the ironworker, the tinsmith, the turner and the carpenter..." (Raymond Chasle, Maisons Traditionelles de l'Ile Maurice*)*

Above: *Unlike the open verandah with its modest and easily movable furniture, the glazed verandah is protected from the vicissitudes of the elements. Its atmosphere is cosy and it lends itself easily to use as a sitting room.*

Right: *This house in Quatre Bornes has belonged to the Moolan family since 1941. The glazed verandah was completely replaced and redecorated in 1950. The woodwork is as fine as lace.*

Left: *Béthanie at Beau-Bassin: its architecture expresses a strong love for sobriety and elegance.*

Above: *Verdun dates from the first years of this century and has remained the property of the Dawood family since 1940. The bow windows were added around 1950. Although the glazing has suffered from many a cyclone the owners have always felt honour-bound to replace it.*

Right: *This house on Shand Street, Beau-Bassin, was constructed during the late ninteenth century.*

Above: *The porch and bow window of Les Palmiers, Phoenix, betray the influence of the British on the architecture of this late ninteenth century house.*
Left: *The outhouses have been converted into a pavilion where guests and relatives can stay.*

"Coffee on the verandah, a deliciously fresh air and bright moonlight; there are moments that repay one for a tropical midday; the evening and the early morning are divine and to see the people sitting listlessly in their deep chairs giving themselves up entirely to the soft languor that then creeps over one, you would think them the most careless beings on earth, as in one sense, perhaps, they are...". The comments of the Bengal Civilian, made in his journal of 1838, are just as applicable to life on the verandah today.

Les Quatre Vents in Moka, with its whitewashed walls, black roof, Wedgewood-blue shutters, long, square-columned verandah and tall French windows, represents all that is most typical of traditional Mauritian architecture. The colours — white, black and Wedgewood blue — were not chosen at random but because they are the colours that were used in the early days of building. Roofs used to be covered in the black bitumen paint used by naval boatbuilders to protect the hulls; walls were whitewashed with lime produced locally by burning madrepores; and the blue of the shutters was achieved by adding permanganate (to protect the wood from termites) to this lime.

Left: *This house on Shand Street, Beau-Bassin, is practically enveloped by a flowering mango tree and a cascade of bougainvillea.*

Right: *Strong sunlight creates a dramatic pattern of white against a dark background. This might explain why decorative detailing is found mostly on the verandah. "There is, when the blinds are down, a bird-cage look about them..." (C S Boyle,* Far Away, or Sketches of Scenery and Society in Mauritius, *1867)*

Headquarters House in Vacoas was built in 1870 by Edmond de Chazal and now belongs to the government. It owes its British colonial look to extensive additions made in 1904. The porch, crowned with a turret, dates from this time. It also has a surprising resemblance to the architecture of certain Caribbean islands. The chimney might seem out of place in a tropical country but in fact it does serve a function in "the highlands" where winter temperatures often fall to 10°C and humidity is high.

Chateau Trompette in Moka was built around 1870 by Mr Janvier Desvaux and was named after the house of the same name in Bordeaux. A British general rented the house in the 1890s and is said to have given grand balls to the rousing sound of military bands. Mr Montocchio who lived in La Malmaison (now the Curepipe Town Hall) moved to Trompette in 1894 with his family of nine children.

"It had those tall doors, half-door and half-window, veiled by muslin curtains with those impossble ornate handles working on rods that you find in French houses. They opened out of all the rooms in all directions and led into all the other rooms." (F. D. Ommaney, The Shoals of Capricorn, *1952)*

The dining room. The huge table used to be laid for the 18 members of the Montocchio family. The brass candelabra was acquired in Europe at the turn of the century. Being extremely farsighted, the owner of the house acquired a duplicate of its opal globe at the same time, and also bought a second, identical tapestry for the drawing room.

The glazed verandah was probably adopted in Mauritius as an extension of the trend for conservatories and glasshouses which spread throughout Europe in the nineteenth century. This type of verandah is a phenonomen particular to the architecture of Mauritius; it is interesting to note that it is rarely seen in other countries that otherwise have a similar style of architecture. On Mauritius, roughly one in three houses have a glazed verandah. They look as if they are hermetically sealed, but, in fact, the small panes can often be opened to ensure a constant flow of air during the summer. These small panes are also able to resist the force of cyclones, whereas large glass windows are fragile and can be dangerous.

Left: *This house in Curepipe exudes an atmosphere of romance despite its worn appearance.*
Above: *Children seem to discover the world leaning out of the window.*

There are some houses whose roofs are of corrugated iron but whose turrets are shingled. Perhaps this is because shingles last longer on steeper roofs? The desire to catch the eye of the passer-by brought more and more decorative detailing to houses on the street. Dormer windows on turrets often had no other function than to embellish the façade of a house. Wood had to be painted so that it would resist bad weather and, often, as in the case of these French windows, it was veined to imitate the natural wood which was so fashionable in Europe during the early years of the twentieth century.

As years went by the smaller houses endeavoured to emulate their forebears, imitating their elegance, their serenity and even the proud dignity of their turrets. The French window was common in modest dwellings as well as grand houses. When the summer heat becomes stifling the openings, always placed opposite each other on the same axis, allow the air to circulate and provide refreshing ventilation.

Sorèze House in Vacoas owes its name to the property of that name at Les Pailles where the house was originally built. It was moved to its present location at the end of the nineteenth century. The large round columns stand like sentinels on the bare verandah of the house.

Above: *"The polished floor, beautiful to look at but dangerous to the equilibrium of the uninitiated…"* (Rev. Beaton, Creoles and Coolies or Five Years in the Mauritius, 1859)

Right: *Note that some of the windows at Sorèze House do not descend to the floor; this affords a better use of space within the house. Although French windows provide ventilation they may, if numerous, make for difficulties in arranging furniture.*

Left: *The varangue at Les Palmiers at Phoenix is laid with traditional stone paving cut from the basalt rock that is found all over the island.*
Above and right: *The timeless and peaceful quality of the verandah at Béthanie is inspired as much by the simple detailing of the columns and balustrade as by the delicacy of the plants and the sophistication of the furniture.*

Left: *This unusual house, probably built around the end of the nineteenth century, exemplifies all the genius of Mauritian craftsmen. It is one of the most intensely decorated houses on the plateau.*

Above and right: *La Sablonnière in Curepipe was built around 1888 by Mr de Chazal. He named it after a family property in Auvergne. The Eiffel Tower in the garden is an exact replica of the Parisian Eiffel Tower and was erected in 1889.*

Overleaf: *These photographs demonstrate the diversity of styles found in the houses of the plateau. Large or small, the options are endless: open or glazed verandahs, hipped or gabled roofs, dormer windows or turrets, one storey or more...*

Left: *During the last decade the façade of this house in Petit Raffray was rebuilt using concrete, but retaining the original roof and turrets. The result is a startling, although not entirely unsuccessful, mixture of styles.*

Below left: *The painter's brush was all that was needed to give this house a new lease of life.*

"What joy it must have been to see the canopies installed, the roof go up, the shingles nailed down, and the decorative trim of the verandah put in its place to balance the rigour of the roof structure...". (Raymond Chasle, Maisons Traditionelles de l'Ile Maurice)

Overleaf: *La Rocherie in Rose Hill was probably built at the end of the nineteenth century. The foundations are built of the same stone as the local church, Notre Dame de Lourdes. Julie Comtesse de Carne lived here for many years before her death in 1986 at the age of 103.*

URBAN ARCHITECTURE

Port-Louis: the capital has always been at the centre of Mauritian life. Originally known as "the Camp", and then as the "Northwest Port", it only became Port-Louis under Labourdonnais. But the name was not final: the town was also known as "Port du Montagne" and, under Decaen an order was passed on 17 August 1906 renaming it "Port Napoleon".

Both capital and commerical centre, Port-Louis' history really began in 1735 with the arrival of Mahé de Labourdonnais. A governor of great genius who combined the roles of architect and engineer, he contrived to build up the town in a very short space of time. However it is to Cossigny, who played his part before the day of Labourdonnais, that we owe the rigour of the town plan established in 1732. The various districts of the town gradually took shape, the size of the grid determining the size of the house. The variety of grid sizes gave the town its well-defined framework of blocks, still in evidence today, and comparable to collection of chessboards of varying sizes.

Most Port-Louis houses are set back from the street in a garden, but there are also small houses built onto the pavement, peculiar only to urban architecture. In the commercial district one comes across boutiques, the ground floor given over to commerce and the first floor to family living.

Towards the end of the nineteenth century urban development began to sprawl out along the roads and railways; today a serpentine development connects Port-Louis and Mahebourg.

Public buildings are usually found within the urban framework. Simple and devoid of decoration they represent a parallel architectural development in Mauritius. Although most homes were built of wood, civil engineers and government officials had greater confidence in stone and this material was generally adopted for all public buildings.

Page 118: *The façade of this office building in Port-Louis is exceptionally austere, with its stonework, heavy door and wrought-iron balustrade.*

Left: *According to legend, Le Réduit was built in 1748 to be a country house for Barthélémy David. In fact, his plans were further reaching: placed between two ravines, the house would serve as a refuge in case of attack by the English. In this very same year, General Boscawen attempted to take the island by surprise and David's work was justified. However, the original wooden building soon fell into disrepair and was rebuilt in stone in 1778 by le Chevalier Guiran de la Brillane.*

Above: *The Temple d'Amour was built by Sir Hesketh Bell (governor from 1916 to 1924) in memory of Barthélémy David.*

Left: *The eye floats gently over the garden to the "Bout du Monde", a breathtaking viewpoint overlooking steep ravines.*
Above: *The rear verandah of Le Réduit is bathed in the golden light of sunset. This house has been compared to a small-scale, tropical Versailles.*

Government House was one of the first buildings to be built by Mahé de Labourdonnais on his arrival in Mauritius in 1735. The second storey was added in 1809 by General Decaen, the last French governor of the island. It has thus been the seat of successive governments: French, British and, since 1968, Mauritian.

When the British forces first arrived in Mauritius in 1810 they built their army barracks on the coast. They were moved from here to Curepipe in 1875 and thence to Vacoas in 1903 as a consequence of the typhoid epidemic of 1890. These buildings are now occupied by the Special Mobile Force of Mauritius. The roof is unusual: instead of the usual shingles, it is covered with asbestos tiles, specially imported from England.

Above: *This detail illustrates features typical of most public buildings in Port-Louis. Built of stone it has wooden shutters, a wrought iron balustrade and decorative trimmings in both metal and wood.*
Right: *Construction of the Mauritius Institute or Port-Louis Museum commenced on 23 November 1880; Governor Bowen laid the first stone. Nowadays it houses a natural history collection, an art gallery and a library.*
Overleaf: *The Flacq Court buildings were built by Governor Archibald Gordon (governor from 1871 to 1874). The architectural design was inspired by his castle in Scotland.*

Above: *This building has been saved from demolition and is now used as offices. Built around 1857 it was the residence of Thomy Thiery until his return to France in 1875. An avid collector, this Mauritian was made Chevalier de la Legion d'Honneur for his work in safeguarding many French treasures. On his death his important collection of works of art went to the Louvre.*
Left: *The cast-iron columns of the verandah are ingeniously designed to serve as rainwater pipes.*

Built around 1823, this house has belonged to the parish of the Immaculate Conception since 1866. Note the balustrade made of oak staves and the old lamp posts that support the pergola. "This building was constructed to resist cyclones as ship resists hurricanes..." (Father Henri Souchon, Vicar of the Immaculate Conception).

Above: *Mon Désir in Port-Louis has resisted the ravages of the humid climate, losing none of its nobility and antiquated charm.*
Left: *The balcony of the Ireland Blyth building in Port-Louis displays typical evidence of the skill of local artisans.*

Right: *As early as 1812 Milbert mentioned the Mauritian practice of converting attic space in gable ends into bedrooms. He also noted that people in the tropics preferred wooden houses to more solid constructions: "Experience has taught them that this kind of building is better suited to the climate. Wood does not conduct heat, allowing it to penetrate only slowly and deflecting most of the light."*

Below right: *"In wood there are latent shapes that can be awakened by the artisan's tool. It is a warm and vibrant material that can become the spirit of a home, and no manmade product will ever replace it. Wood talks and sings and works; it has a presence of its own." (Bernard Clavel).*

Mon Rêve, residence of Mlle Adèle, was built before the cyclone of 1892. It was bought by Mr Adèle, the father of the present owner, in 1911. It was he who closed the verandah on both sides, built the wall and gate and, in 1925, added a second storey.

Above: *The famous Wedgewood blue, so loved by Mauritians, has been used to decorate the interior of this bedroom.*
Left: *Often seen on the verandah, the polished red floor — or châlis — probably originates from India. In more modest abodes this style of floor may be adopted throughout the house.*

Since the death of Mlle Adèle's mother, almost fifty years ago, this room has remained unchanged. All of the furniture was ordered by her father in 1908 and made by a Mauritian joiner, Mr Sandivi. His workshop used to be next to the theatre in Port-Louis.

Above: *The bedroom is a repository for religious icons and all kinds of family memorabilia, the kind of room that is "reminiscent of the white walls of the seminary and the mass..." (Loys Masson, Les autres nourritures).*
Left: *The terracotta statue representing the muse Sapho was purchased by Mlle Adèle's father on a trip to France.*

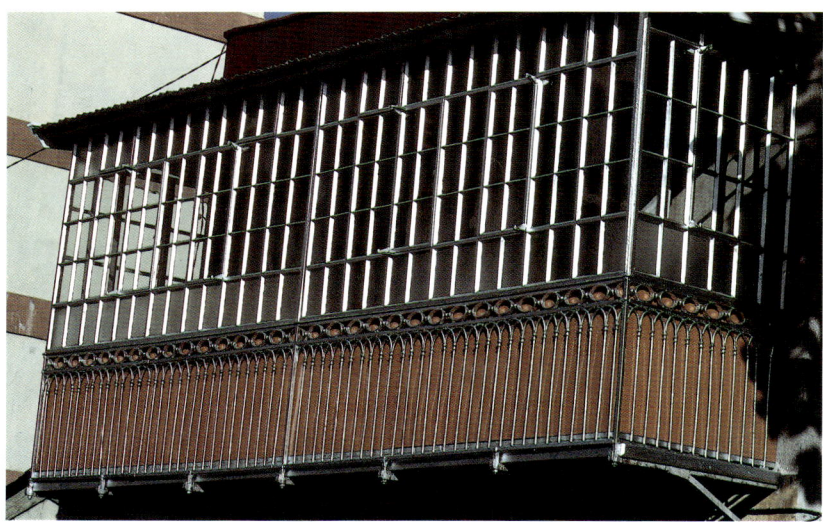

Above: *Town houses are usually set in walled gardens or courtyards amongst large trees that provide ample shade. Yet space is still at a premium. Whilst people living in the highlands could easily extend their houses by adding a wing to the side or the back, the people of Port-Louis had only one option: to convert the roof. The design is always simple, providing a comfortable living area within.*

Left: *This balcony, originally looking straight onto the road in Port-Louis, has been enclosed with glass.*

On 6 June 1769, the day of his arrival in Mauritius, then the Ile de France, Mr Desroches (governor from 1769 to 1772) made the first proclamation regarding the appearance of the capital. Inhabitants were hitherto obliged to enclose their house or land with a wall or, failing that, with a living hedge of bamboo, acacia, or other prickly bush. Fences made of palisades, planks or any other kind of dead wood were forbidden. Every owner should plant on his land eleven trees, such as tamarind, mango or peach trees, at intervals that were prescribed according to the acreage of the land in question. According to Governor Desroches, a place as hot as the town of Port-Louis, denuded of greenery for most of the year, produced a sad and unattractive impression (A Toussaint, Port-Louis: deux siècles d'histoire*).*

These small urban houses are built right on the pavement are typical of Port-Louis. This simple style of architecture has long been in existence and has often been depicted in old prints and engravings.

"Yoloffs Street". The name of this street is not fortuitous: it has definite historical origins. In the days of French rule the town of Port-Louis was divided into three sections: the town centre, the western district and the eastern district. One of the areas within the eastern district was known as "Camp Yoloff" because it was the home of the descendants of the Yoloffs from Senegal.

Left: *Modern day Port-Louis has been invaded by motorcycles, lorries and cars, and yet handcarts are still used to transport merchandise.*

Right: *Two-storey boutiques, such as this one in Beau Bassin, are sometimes found outside Port-Louis. The shop is on the ground floor and the family lives above.*

Below right: *Corrugated iron is often used on walls instead of wooden planks.*

The "boutique", equivalent to the corner shop, is found all over the island of Mauritius. Its merchandise varies according to the means of the owner and to its location. Some boutiques only sell the bare necessities whilst others have an amazingly colourful profusion of disparate wares, worthy of an Ali Baba's cave. As well as pots of jam, there are babies' bottles and dominos, plaster models of the well-loved Father Laval (priest of Mauritius) and coconut brooms, and all the usual small goods of the ironmonger, such as nails and glue... The boutique will allow the customer to buy in bulk or on credit but it is also a place where you can by a single cigarette, a candle or a sardine sandwich.

The boutique is at the heart of Mauritian daily life. It is a social place where men gather while the women look after the home. Outside the boutique street vendors gather to sell their pistachios, spicy sweets, samosas and other snacks, knowing that here they have a guaranteed market for their wares.

The magnificent Episcopal Palace is the creation of master builders Darode and Gilbert. Its construction was a major project: work started in April 1847 and lasted until October 1852.

This is a typical commercial boutique in Port-Louis, characterised by colourful walls and shutters. Sadly, unless demolition and redevelopment are controlled, buildings such as this are doomed.

Poncini, the well-known Port-Louis store, has held out steadfastly against the concrete invasion. The startlingly Parisian street lamp in the foreground was a replacement for the miniature Eiffel Tower (presented at the Universal Exhibition of Paris in 1889) which stood here before being moved to La Sablonnière at Curepipe.

Although no-one knows the exact date of construction of this building on the Place des Armes, Port-Louis, records show that the Oriental Banking Corporation operated here during the years between 1852 and 1885. It is now the premises of the Hong Kong Bank. The red-roofed building in the background dates from the very first years of the French colony on Mauritius. Once the bakery that provided bread and biscuits for fleets en route for the West Indies, it is now the home of the national mint. The Place des Armes has preserved all its old-world charm and, up to now, no sky-scraper has broken the harmony of its architecture.

Left: *Built at the beginning of the twentieth century, this charming house in Phoenix was originally the station master's house. In 1964, when the railways became redundant, it became the meeting-place for scuba-divers belonging to the Mauritius Underwater Group.*

Right: *Bowen Square, Port Louis. A fountain dating from 1915 stands in front of the Ireland Blyth building. During 1989, the Year of the Environment, this square was totally renovated.*

Above: *Jules Leclerc once said that if Mauritius is the paradise of the southern hemisphere, the Pamplemousses gardens are the paradise of Mauritius...*
Left: *These giant water lilies are the gardens' major attraction. They open in the afternoon and close the following morning. On the first day they are white, and on the second they are pink.*

Labourdonnais purchased the Mon Plaisir Estate in 1735 and created a kitchen garden that should provide for his staff, for the growing population of Port-Louis and for the crews of passing ships. The Pamplemousses Gardens were originally conceived as a nursery where plants of botanical or economic interest imported from Europe or the East could be acclimatised. In 1768 Mon Plaisir was sold to M. Poivre. It was he, in fact, who was the true creator of the Pamplemousses Gardens: under his ownership they became a centre of exchange for plants from all around the world. The grandiose entrance gates, funded by public money, were installed in 1868.

Above: *The mountains of Mauritius have always impressed travellers, inspiring descriptions such as "vast pocket Matterhorns" or "fantastic peaks...as if nature had been in a merry mood at the time of their creation".*

Left: *Sugar harvesting has always been hard manual labour; the introduction of machines is a comparatively recent event.*

Above: *Situated at the entrance to Port-Louis, the Koenig Tower is built of the volcanic stone that is found all over Mauritius. Farmers try to clear their land of this stone, and the small pyramids that they build in the cane fields have become a feature of the Mauritian landscape.*
Above right: *One can almost hear the crackle of burning cane, a practice that facilitates harvesting.*
Right: *The primitive ox-drawn cart is a rare sight in the days of the modernised sugar industry.*
Overleaf: *Curepipe Town Hall. To love a house is to strive for its survival and to give it a new lease of life.*

'CAMPEMENTS' AND HOTELS

The rustle of the filaos trees, the lapping of the waves...here, in the most perfect surroundings, one comes across the *campement* made of ravenala with its roof of straw, symbol of a bygone age.

The joys of the coast were discovered at the turn of the century when the eradication of malaria and the arrival of the motorcar combined to stimulate development in areas previously inaccessible and considered to be insalubrious. Mauritians began to spend the winter months in rudimentary dwellings known as "campements". They used to bring almost all household goods for the "season", this giving birth to the expression "going camping...".

A whole generation of Mauritians still remembers the palava of setting off. Under the vigilant eye of the mistress of the house the ox-drawn carts are numbered and their contents listed: chairs, mattresses, small pieces of furniture, kitchen implements and clothing, not forgetting the chicken coops. The convoy moves off at about eight o'clock and heads for the coast. Soon afterwards the members of the family, all of whom have been ready for hours, pile into the car to follow the same route. Children crave for that first heady smell of the sea. The car will reach its destination first, and only when, late in the afternoon, the carts finally arrive, has the season truly begun.

The post-war period witnessed the disappearance of the traditional style of building; it was replaced by a modern architecture which paid no attention to the lessons learnt in the previous two hundred and fifty years of living in Mauritius. Only in the past ten years has there been a return to traditional architecture and an attempt to marry its most appealing elements with contemporary technology and the demands of a modern way of life. Whereas Mauritian architecture developed primarily for residential needs, it is to the hotels that we owe our renewed architectural identity. It would seem that this reemergence of the importance of heritage has intensified: today's new buildings are conceived in traditional Mauritian style, and traditional features are incorporated in modern houses. At long last, the virtues of the verandah have been rediscovered.

Page 160: *"We, the children of Mauritius, slumber in a cradle rocked by the waves of the Indian Ocean just within the tropics…"* (C J Boyle, Far Away, or Sketches of Scenery and Society in Mauritius, *1867*). Above and left: *In 1989, Mauritians celebrated the 350th anniversary of the introduction of deer to the island (8 November 1639). The deer were imported from Indonesia and set free at the foot of the Montagne du Lion. There are accounts by Milbert from as early as 1804 describing hunting parties that lasted for more than a week.*

Above: *The memoirs of the fanatical Alfred Montocchio mention the elation of seeing a trophy, even years after it was taken.*
Above right: *These twining branches are called "liane de cerf". They are often used as balustrades for hunting lodges, or "campements de chasse", as they are known locally.*
Right: *The old oil lamp and copper water tank are vestiges of the days of the primitive, yet comfortable, hunting lodges.*

Above: *La Hutte in Trou d'Eau Douce was built in 1906 by Henri Leclezio, the owner of Euréka. Destroyed by cyclone Carol in 1960, it was subsequently rebuilt on its existing foundations.*

Left: *The construction of the roof is visible from the inside. The thatch is attached to the wood-and-bamboo structure with rope made of coconut fibres.*

Right: *A contemporary extension has been added to a traditional campement: the walls are of concrete but the roof is of ravenala. The glazed verandah serves as a corridor between the two parts of the house, protecting the inmates from the strong trade winds.*

Below right: *Many of the traditional campements on the east coast of the island have no verandah on the seaward side as it is uncomfortable to sit outside during the winter months. The casuarina trees, known locally as "filaos", form an integral part of the seaside landscape.*

How many times have these walls heard the story of seven deer killed by seven shots...? A single glance at a trophy will bring back all the memories of where a certain stag was shot and how he fell.

Above: *The Domaine de Chasseur, opened in 1988, is a park where the public can go shooting or hiking and can even eat and stay the night.*

Right: *This tree fern of the genus* Cyathea, *known locally as "fandia", is a protected species.*

Left: *In contrast to the usual light rattan furniture of the verandah, this incongruous mixture of objects creates a cosy atmosphere of permanence.*
Above: *Until 1860 when gas was introduced to Mauritius, lamps such as this were fuelled by sperm whale oil.*

Above: *"The mosquito net barely protected me from the greedy hum of mosquitoes..."* (Arthur Martial, Sphinx de Bronze).
Right: *The interior of a campement is often dark due to the use of ravenala, to the stained wooden beams (black varnish prevents termite attack) and to the dark red châlis. Until relatively recently campements were used only as holiday homes and their construction was rudimentary.*

This campement in Trou d'Eau Douce is an invitation to wallow in sweet idleness. It is easy to imagine a family group reclining languidly in deep armchairs in the shade of the broad verandah. Although inadequate in the high humidity of the plateau, thatched roofs often feature amongst houses on the coast. They have to be replaced (assuming that they are not destroyed by a cyclone) every twenty years or so.

Right: *Like the large house on the plantation, the campement may also have its pavilion to accommodate the all the members of large families.*
Below right: *The palm tree, heavy with coconuts, adds the seal of exoticism to the luxuriant tropical garden.*

Ideally situated on the beach, La Maison looks out over the ever-changing hues of the ocean towards the northern islands. Inaugurated at the end of 1987, it is a luxurious and elegant traditional-style villa where people can stay throughout the year. Overleaf: This moorish-style house on the small island known as "l'Ilot Cocos" in Blue Bay was built by Sir Hesketh Bell (governor from 1916 to 1924).

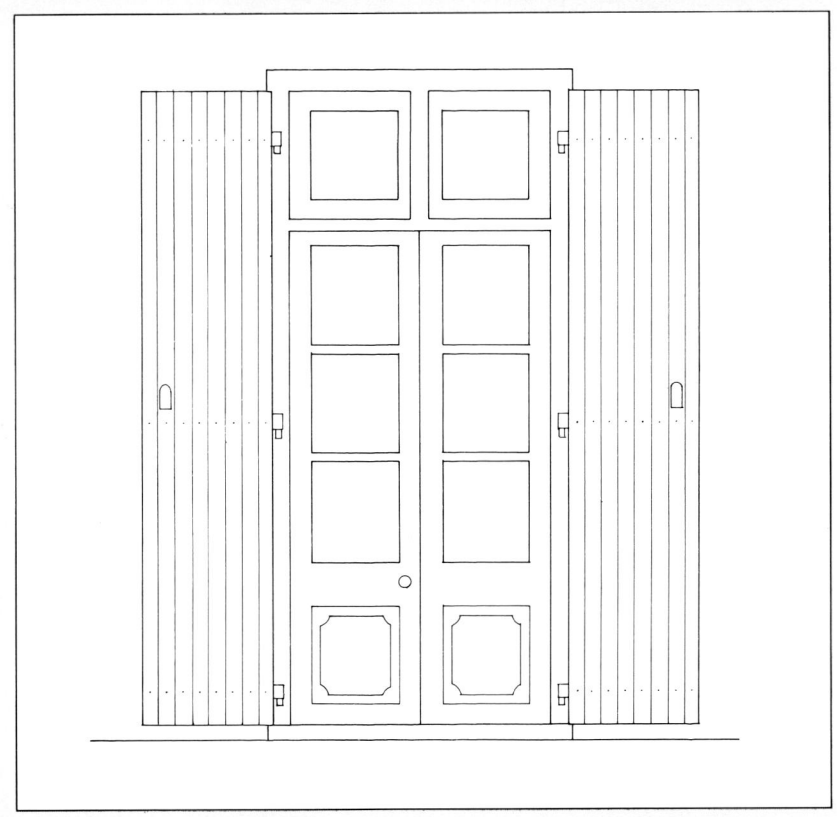

ARCHITECTURAL NOTEBOOK

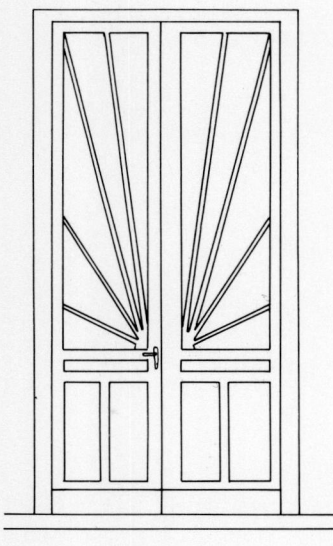

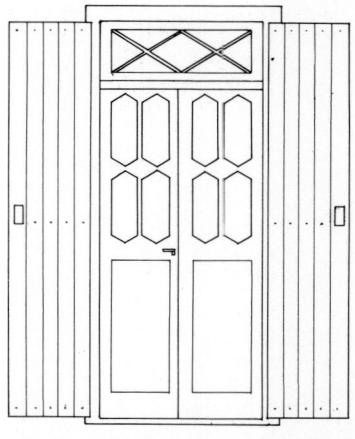

They are in such perfect harmony with their surroundings that one wonders which came first: nature or the houses. Be they large or small, they are a living testimony to a way of life well adapted to the social and climatic conditions of the island. They are unique in the world: a synthesis of all the social and architectural trends that have affected Mauritius over the years of its development.

The sense of magic that emanates from Mauritian traditional architecture evolved slowly from the primitive stone or wooden houses of the first French settlers, each generation providing its contribution. Nobody can state with certainty who exactly contributed those particular features - the verandah, the turrets, the balustrades, the auvents or the decorative ironwork. The cultural and ethnic diversity of the population of Mauritius can be felt intensely in its traditional houses.

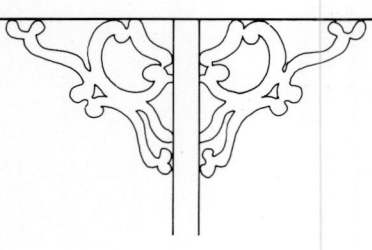

EARLY DAYS 1715-1820

By the eighteenth century, the Mauritian economy was only just taking shape and the early dwellings were primitive. Mahé de Labourdonnais (governor of the island from 1735 to 1747) tried to persuade the settlers to improve their houses and went as far as providing them with the necessary materials and craftsmen.

The first settlers sought to transplant something of what they had left in France to their new land. Mongoust (demolished in 1912) demonstrated clearly their sentimental attachment to their homeland. Similarly, having abandoned their estates in France, Le Juge de Segrais and his family built a "little Segrais" in Mauritius. But whereas the Château de Segrez was designed by an architect and built by specialist craftsmen, Mongoust was the work of the settlers themselves. "Entirely of wood, this dwelling was a true manor house, a vast rectangular building on two floors... it was sombre in style, with good proportions, it contained no colonial features, and with its large cornice and classical detailing it showed all the

*Built in 1803, demolished in 1912 :
"...This dwelling was a true manor house, a vast rectangular building on two floors. It was 21 metres long and 15.50 meters wide, built on a high stone podium which surrounded it on all sides. The entrances were approached by two large flights of twelve steps on both the main façades."
René Le Juge de Segrais, in his* Souvenirs de Segrais et de Mongoust, *relates the poignant story of the demolition of the house : "He (Léonce Le Juge) died only a few days after consenting to the sale of the house at the end of December 1912. It was bought by a developer whose intention was to demolish the house, sell the wood and parcel up the land. A year later it was a 'fait accompli': not a stone or board was left of the venerated house, not a tree, nor even a seed remained of the old orchards."*

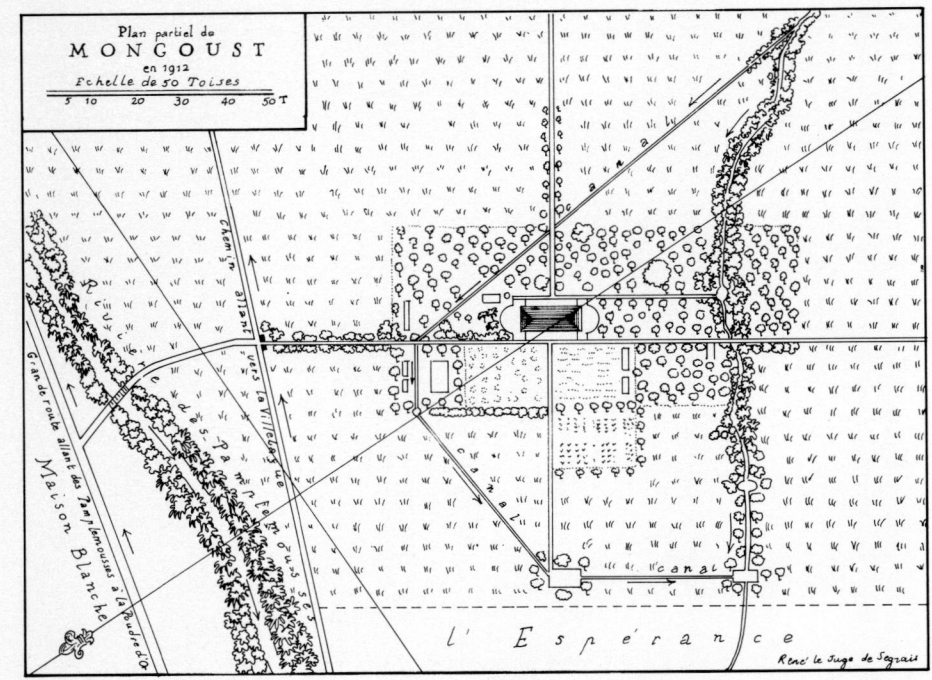

MONGOUST
*Location plan
Front elevation*

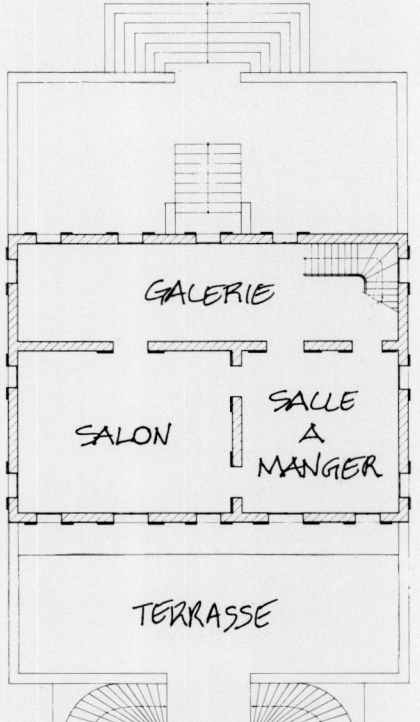
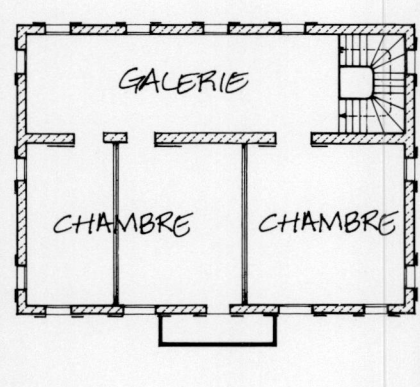

MAHEBOURG MUSEUM
(the historic house of Grand Port)
Front elevation
Plan

characteristics of a French abode of the XVIIIth century..." (René Le Juge de Segrais, *Souvenirs de Segrais et de Mongoust*, 1936). The houses of this period were probably built with the help of French naval carpenters whom Mahé de Labourdonnais had brought with him to build and repair ships. It is thus not surprising that the principles and techniques of naval architecture can be identified in many traditional houses.

Both houses illustrated below have roofs which can be compared to an upturned boat, the structure designed to withstand the force of the wind rather than that of water.

Even in the earliest days, shingles were used on the roofs of wooden houses. Delicate wooden slats thinned at one end were nailed onto a wooden structure. They were then covered with a thick coating of tar-based paint, comparable to that used in boat-building, which rendered them waterproof.

At that time, the development of an architectural style was taking place mainly in Port-Louis (where the town plan designed by Cossigny formed the basis for town planning). There were no villages; the settlers lived far away from one another on their plantations called *défrichés*, like islands in the middle of the vast expanse of tropical forest.

In 1771 Jean de Robillard purchased some land and built the house that was to become the residence of successive commanders of the Grand-Port district and that is now the Mahébourg Museum. Jean de Robillard died in 1809; the following year his widow and children were to provide a refuge for the two illustrious wounded soldiers of the Battle of Grand-Port (23-26 August 1810). The French Captain Duperre and the English Captain Willoughby were cared for in the same room. The government of Mauritius acquired the house in 1947. It was transformed into a naval and historic museum and was opened to the public on 1 September 1950.

THE BIRTH OF MAURITIAN STYLE 1820-1860

By the beginning of the nineteenth century French and English settlers had realised that they should adapt their architecture to the climatic and social conditions of the tropics. All buildings from then on followed a certain number of established rules. Houses were generally made of wood on a stone foundation, the latter shielding the wooden structure from direct contact with the ground and helping with the ventilation. Their height also gave them a commanding position. Stone was generally reserved for administrative buildings and wood was used for residential purposes (the former being very difficult to use; furthermore, local mortar was not easy to mix).

The standard plan is very simple, with all rooms inter-communicating. The living room often occupies the whole depth of the house. Windows are replaced by doors, usually placed on the same axis for easier cross-ventilation.

The main building contains the living room, dining room and bedrooms. The kitchen and bathrooms are normally separate structures at the back of the house. Small pavilions were often found in the garden with additional bedrooms to cater for the larger families and their frequent guests.

Around the main structure is the verandah, an independent feature which runs on one or more sides of the house. The roof of the verandah is flat and commonly known as "argamasse", from the Portuguese word *argamassa* denoting a cement made from crushed tiles and lime. In Mauritius the recipe of argamasse was more complicated and apparently contained, apart from lime, a mixture of eggs, sugar and other exotic ingredients. This paste, perfected by the Indian craftsmen, was so hard that it was very resistant to water and lasted a long time. However, argamasse was soon to be replaced by corrugated iron.

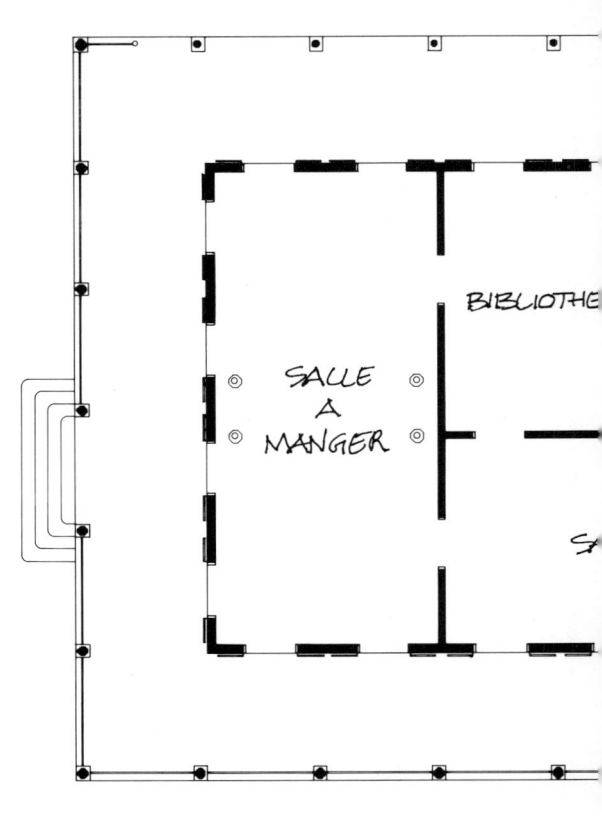

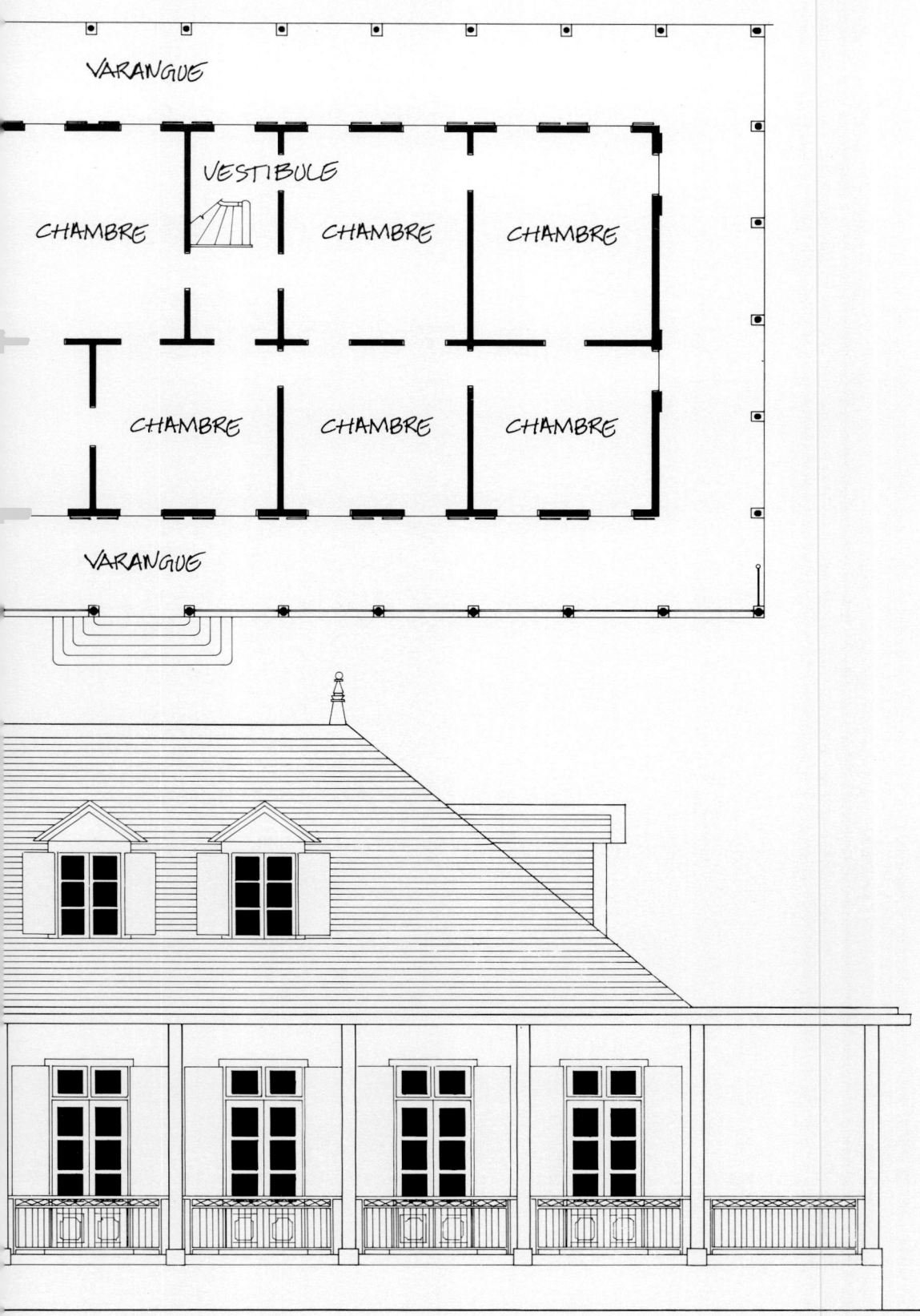

The verandah insulates the main body of the building: it prevents the sun from shining directly into the house and keeps the rain at bay. Furthermore, it solves the problem of communication since it provides direct access to the main rooms of the house. The verandah is a pleasant place to be at all times of the day and is normally the coolest and best lit part of the house, since the rooms are permanently plunged in semi-obscurity. In a country where hospitality is a way of life it becomes an important social feature : "...It is at the same time a noble entrance to the house, a porch... and a place of leisure for rest and social small talk..." (Preliminary studies on traditional housing in Reunion Island)

Nobody would pretend that the verandah is a Mauritian invention. It exists under various other names all over the world - "galerie", "piazza", "porch" - and epitomises a way of life for Europeans who settled abroad. In Mauritius, it is interesting to note that the inclusion of verandahs in residential designs became widespread under the British occupation which began in 1810, and this would seem to indicate the influence of other British colonies.

One could say that the verandah is the most typical feature of the Mauritian house. For those living in the tropics it is as important as is the hearth to those in the northern hemisphere.

EUREKA
Plan and front elevation
Built in 1830 by Mr Carr, it was bought by Mr Eugène LeClézio in 1856, and remained the property of his family until February 1985. Originally its grounds covered 225 acres of garden and forest, but they are now reduced to 5 acres.

EUREKA
Side elevation

CHAMPROSAY IN BEAU BASSIN
Front elevation
Built around 1850 by an Englishman, and now owned by M. Loïs le Vieux.

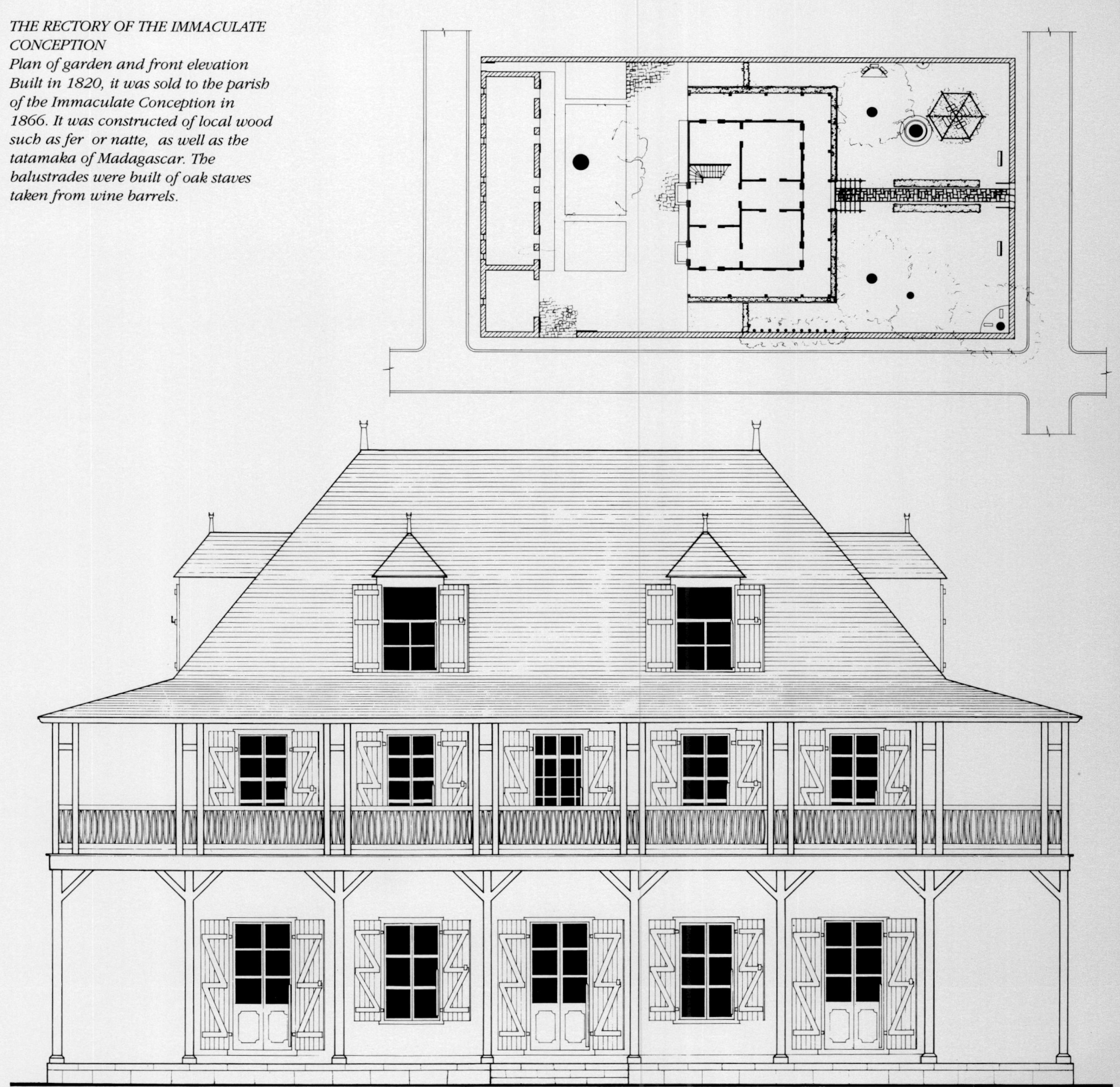

THE RECTORY OF THE IMMACULATE CONCEPTION
*Plan of garden and front elevation
Built in 1820, it was sold to the parish of the Immaculate Conception in 1866. It was constructed of local wood such as fer or natte, as well as the tatamaka of Madagascar. The balustrades were built of oak staves taken from wine barrels.*

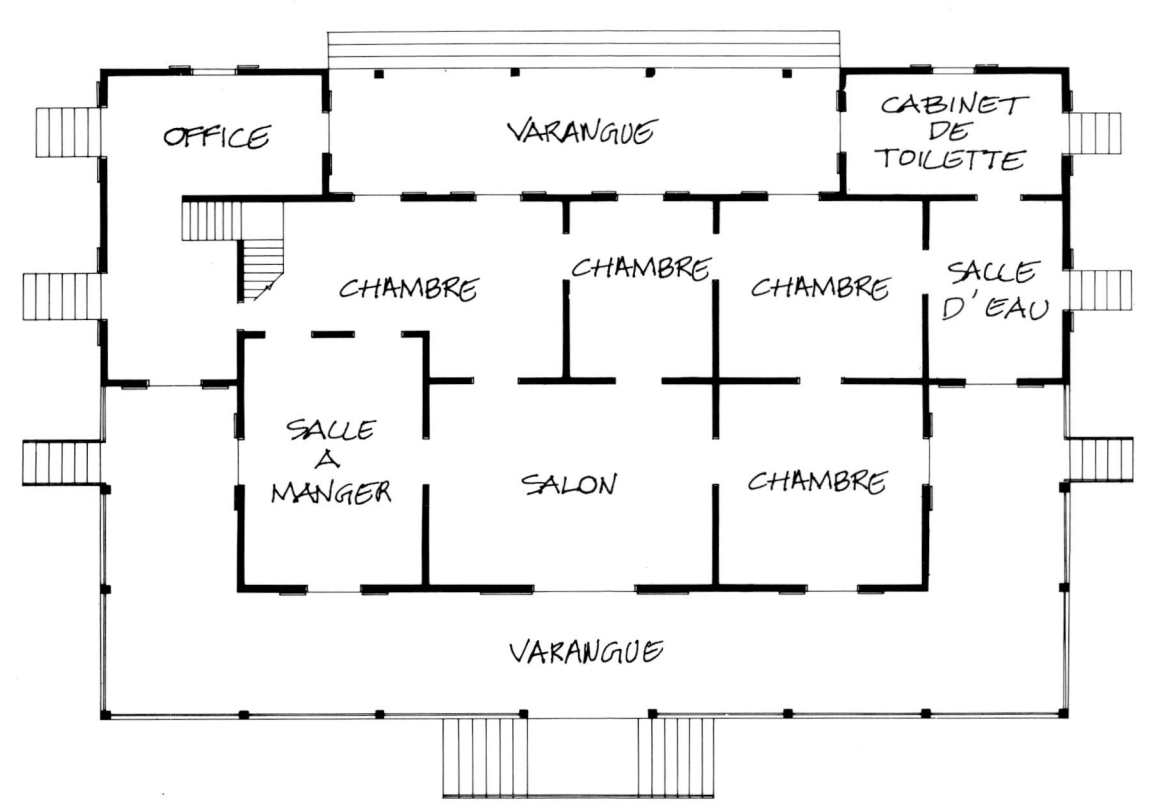

LES QUATRE VENTS
Plan and front elevation
Opposite : general view
Built around 1860. The plan shows the house as it existed in 1930, but it is likely that it was originally designed with a circular verandah.

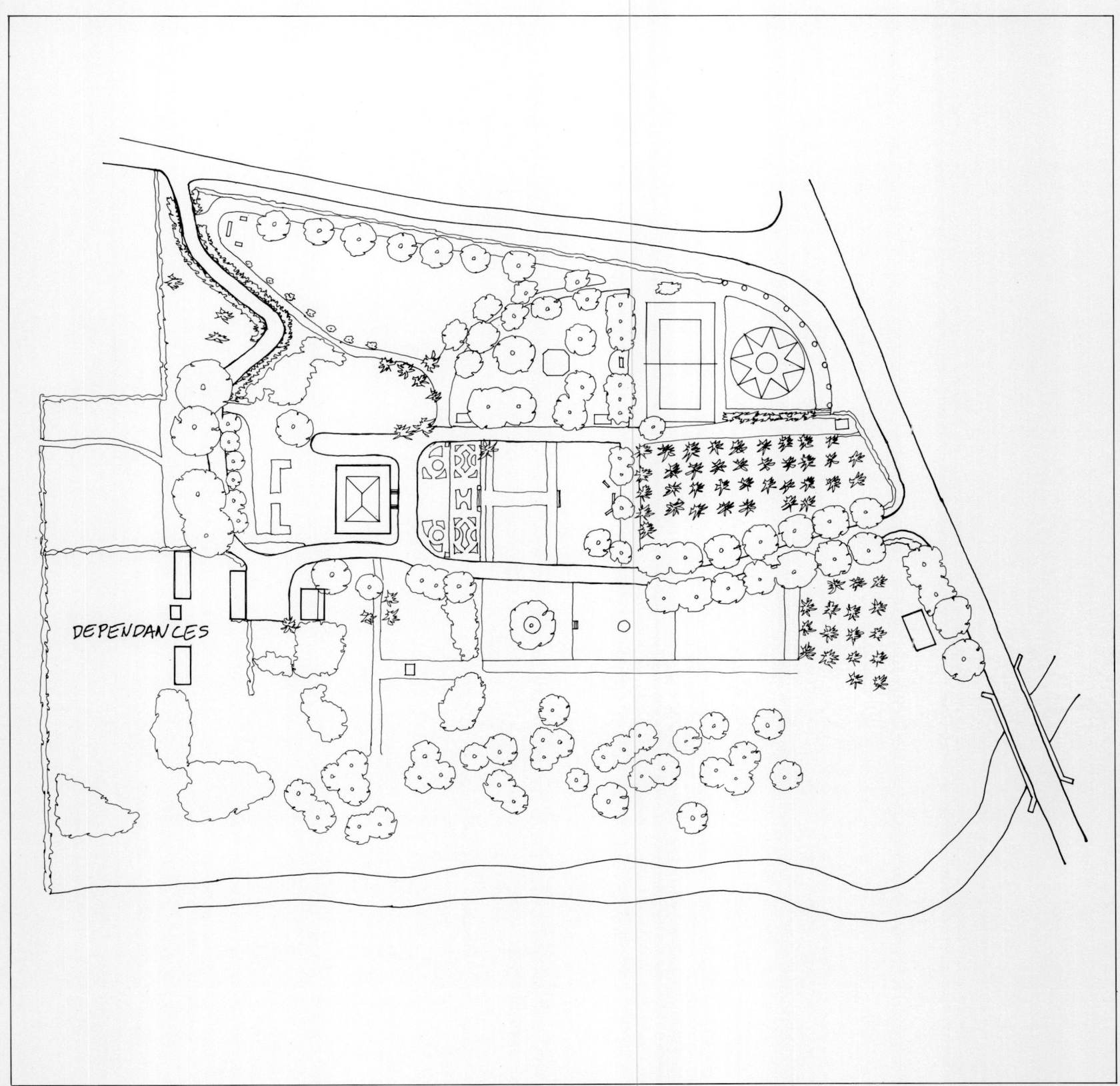

THE ROMANTIC YEARS 1860-1930

The malaria epidemics which coincided with the opening of the railways drove many families to leave Port-Louis for the healthier climate of the central plateau.

A whole series of towns and villages of residential nature gradually took shape with the railways providing a much-improved means of transport for building materials. Although many inhabitants dismantled their houses and rebuilt them on the highlands, Port-Louis remained the commercial and administrative centre.

Having mastered the techniques of the Mauritian style, the settlers could now afford to give free rein to their imagination. Thus, the romantic years saw the introduction of glazed verandahs, a multitude of roof silhouettes, turrets, windows with auvents, bow windows and, overall, an abundance of fanciful decoration.

This was a far cry from those first houses made of rough wooden planks. Not only did the house have to be comfortable but it also had to reflect the social status of its owner: the front façade and, therefore, the verandah were of utmost importance.

There are three distinct styles of verandahs: the verandah with large colonnades, the verandah with balustrades and more complex designs and decorations (these two styles often being seen together) and, finally, the glazed verandah. The latter is found in all parts of the island and even on the cooler upper plains, which would lead us to suppose that it was a social phenomenon rather than a result of climatic conditions.

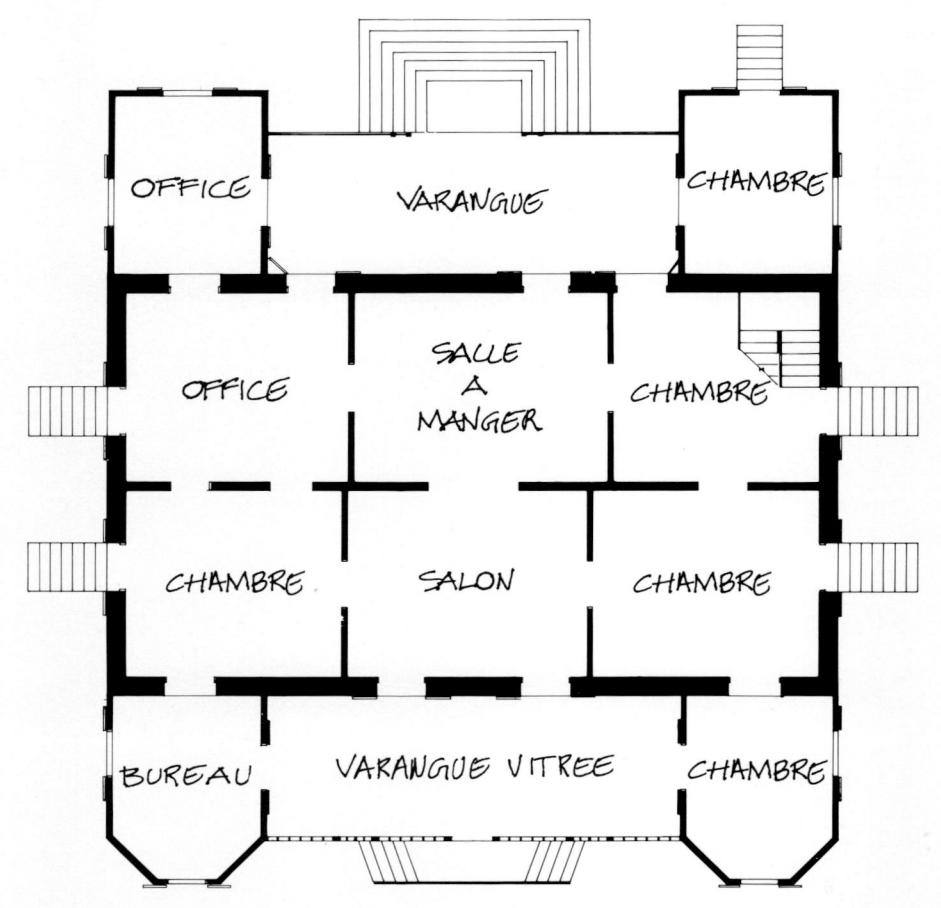

SURPRISE IN MOKA
Front elevation and plan
The main core of the house probably dates from before 1865. The turrets and the glazed verandah were subsequent additions.

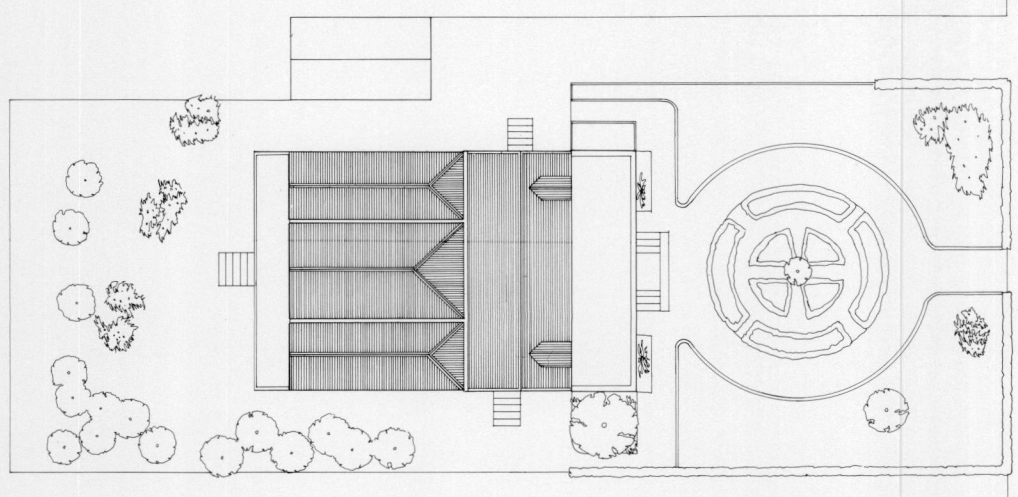

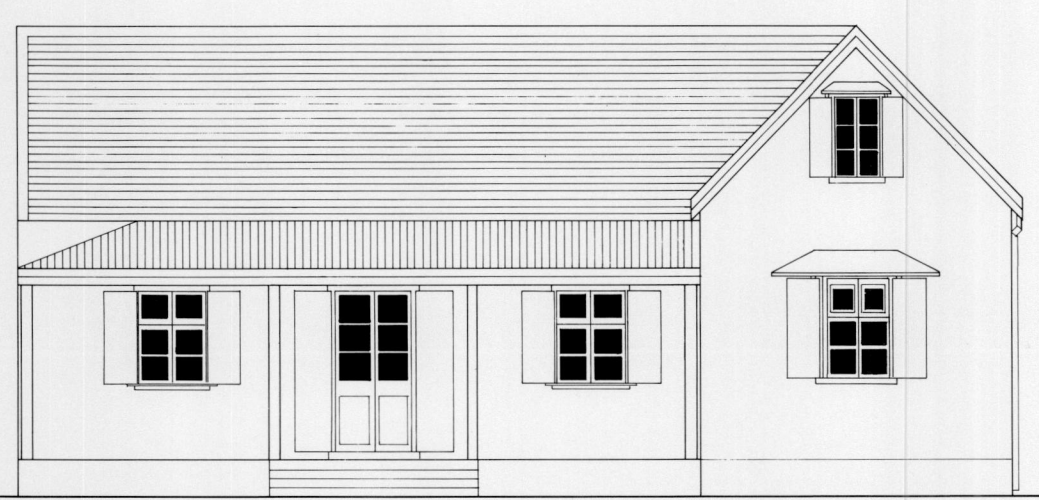

This was the era of Victorian exuberance, and of the bourgeois villas of nineteenth century France. Under British rule, the franco-Mauritian population was able to maintain its traditions and, yet, no one can be certain of the origin of any particular feature. For example, the glazed verandah could well be a version of the English conservatory which was very much in fashion in the nineteenth century, but it is equally true that the *jardin d'hiver* existed at the same time in France.

A major change which took place at that time was the shape of the roof. The hipped roof that covered all the rooms like the hull of an upturned boat was replaced by a whole series of smaller roofs, usually gabled. Here, there is a parallel with Caribbean architecture. The hipped roof is found only in the French West Indies. This would suggest that the introduction of multiple roof silhouettes was the result of British influence.

During this period the rigour and simplicity that characterised early houses were replaced by a more elaborate and complex form of architecture that was, nonetheless, based on the earlier model. There was greater freedom to create and innovate according to one's whims and fancies.

HOUSE IN ST JULIEN D'HOTMAN
Front elevation and plan of the garden
The date of construction is unknown but it is likely to have been built at the turn of the century.

HOUSE AT LE REDUIT
Front elevation
Built in 1908 on government orders with funds given by the sugar industry. It was to house one of the research workers from the bacteriological laboratory that was built at the same time.

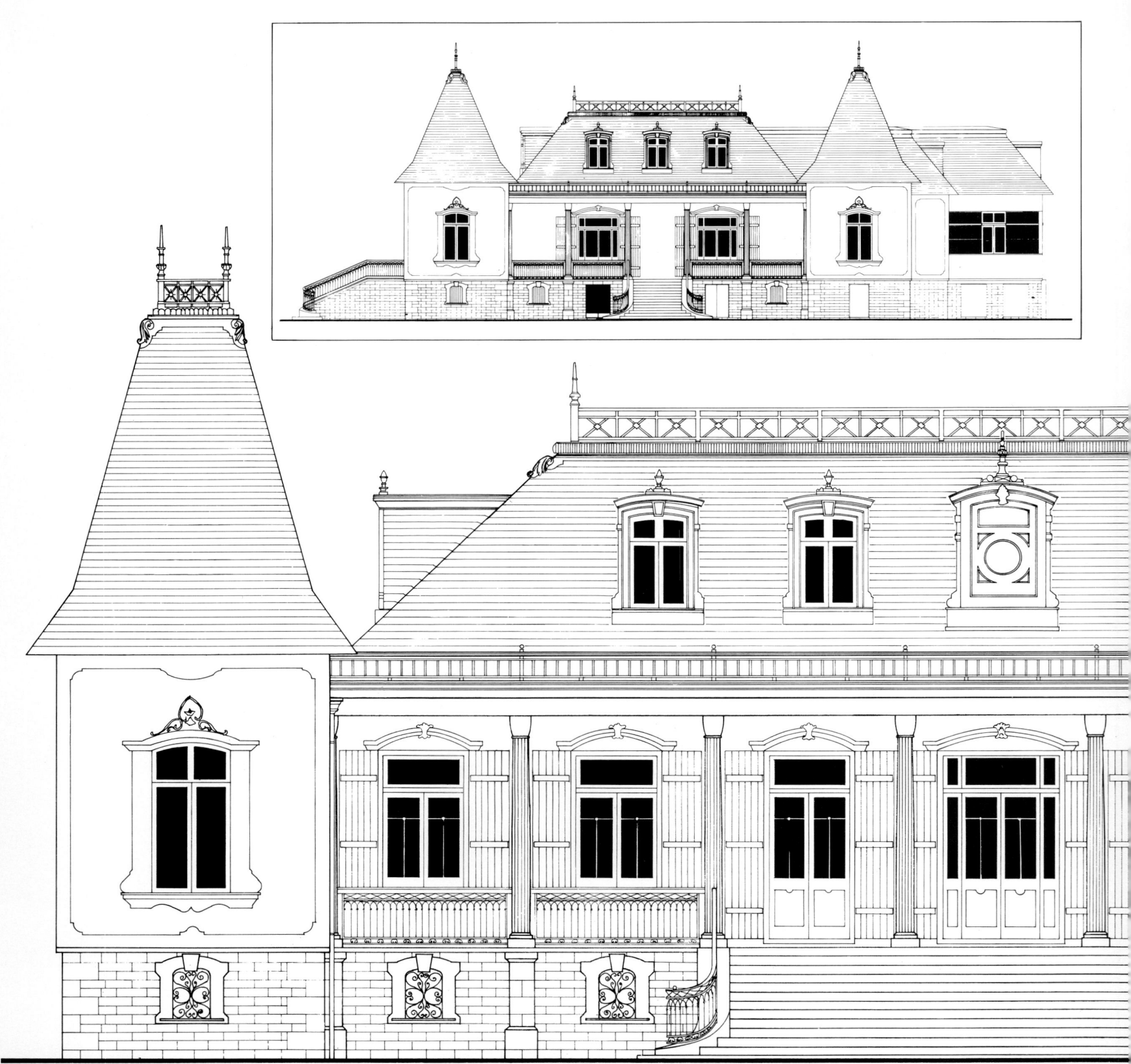

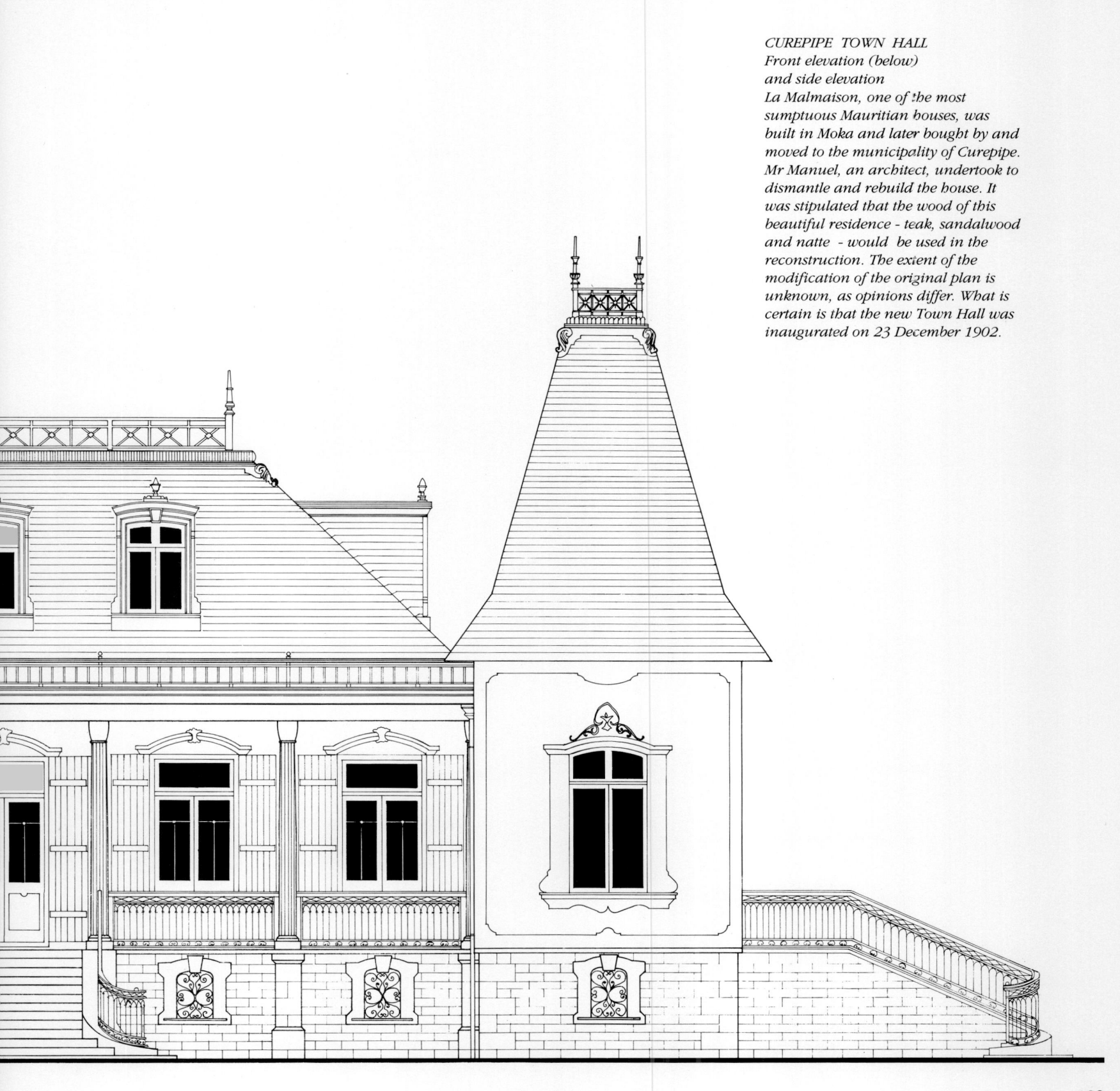

CUREPIPE TOWN HALL
*Front elevation (below)
and side elevation
La Malmaison, one of the most sumptuous Mauritian houses, was built in Moka and later bought by and moved to the municipality of Curepipe. Mr Manuel, an architect, undertook to dismantle and rebuild the house. It was stipulated that the wood of this beautiful residence - teak, sandalwood and natte - would be used in the reconstruction. The extent of the modification of the original plan is unknown, as opinions differ. What is certain is that the new Town Hall was inaugurated on 23 December 1902.*

GNUDI HOUSE, VACOAS
*Front elevation and plan
Built in 1939. The presence of the
British army forces in Vacoas
encouraged the development of the
land surrounding the barracks which
would suggest that the house was built
by an Englishman.*

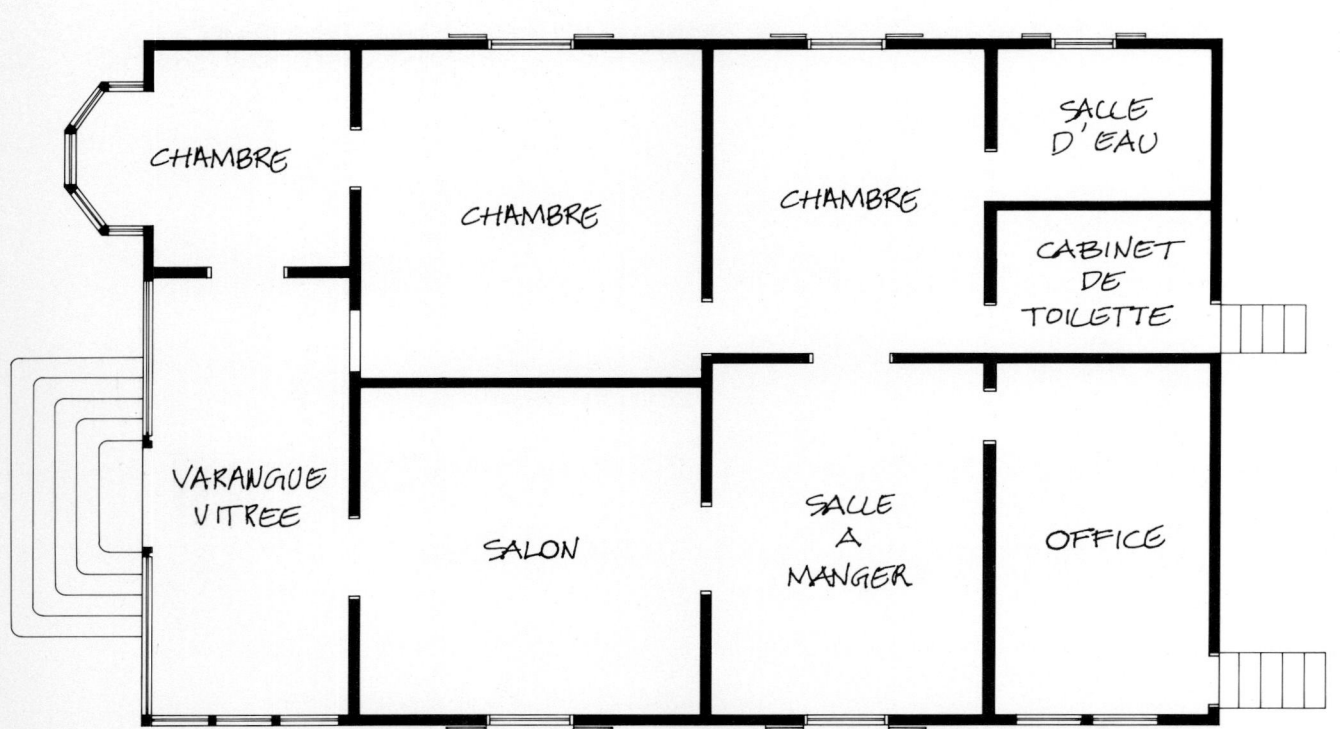

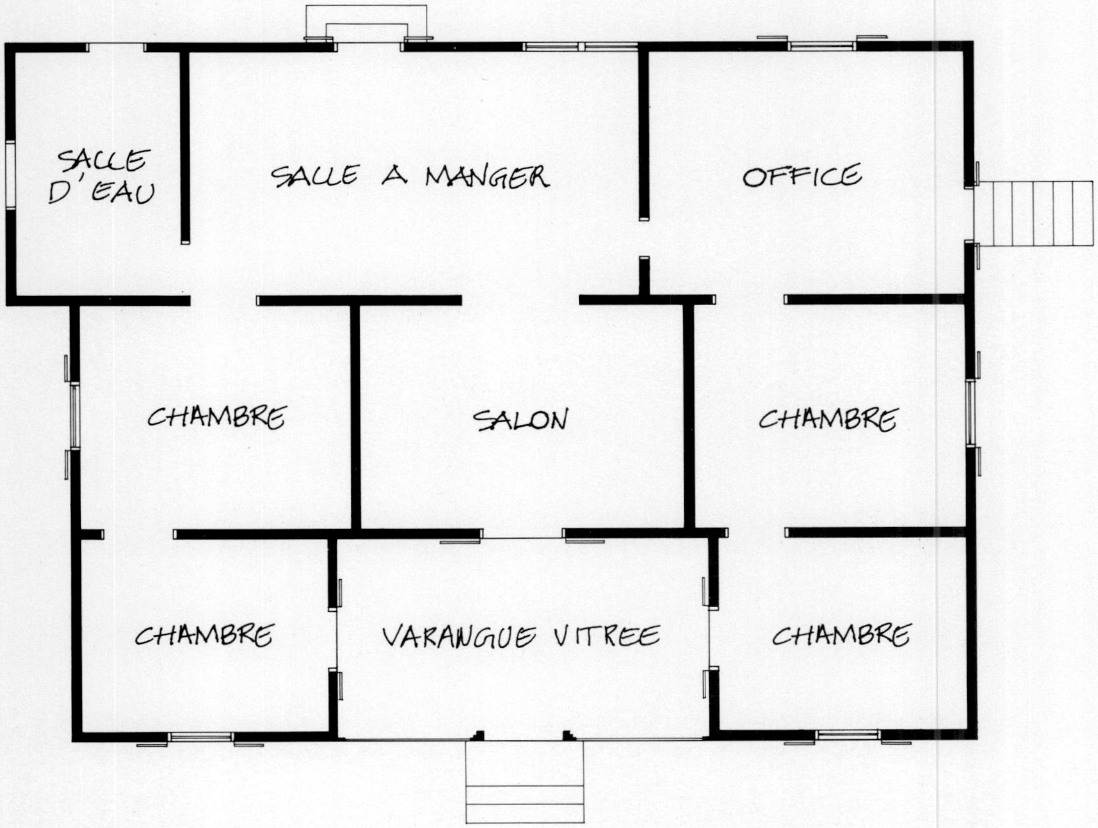

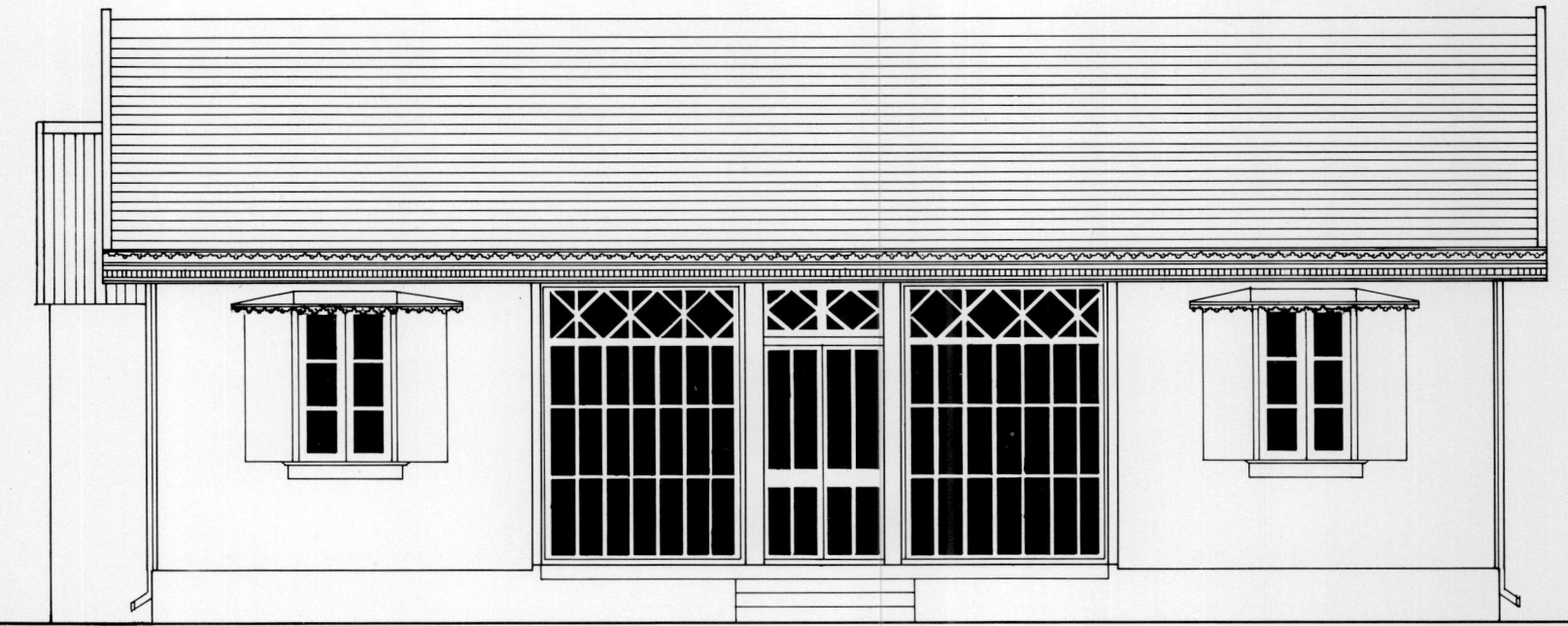

FORT-STEPHENS HOUSE IN VACOAS
Plan and front elevation
Built by an Englishman around 1920. There was an identical house next door.

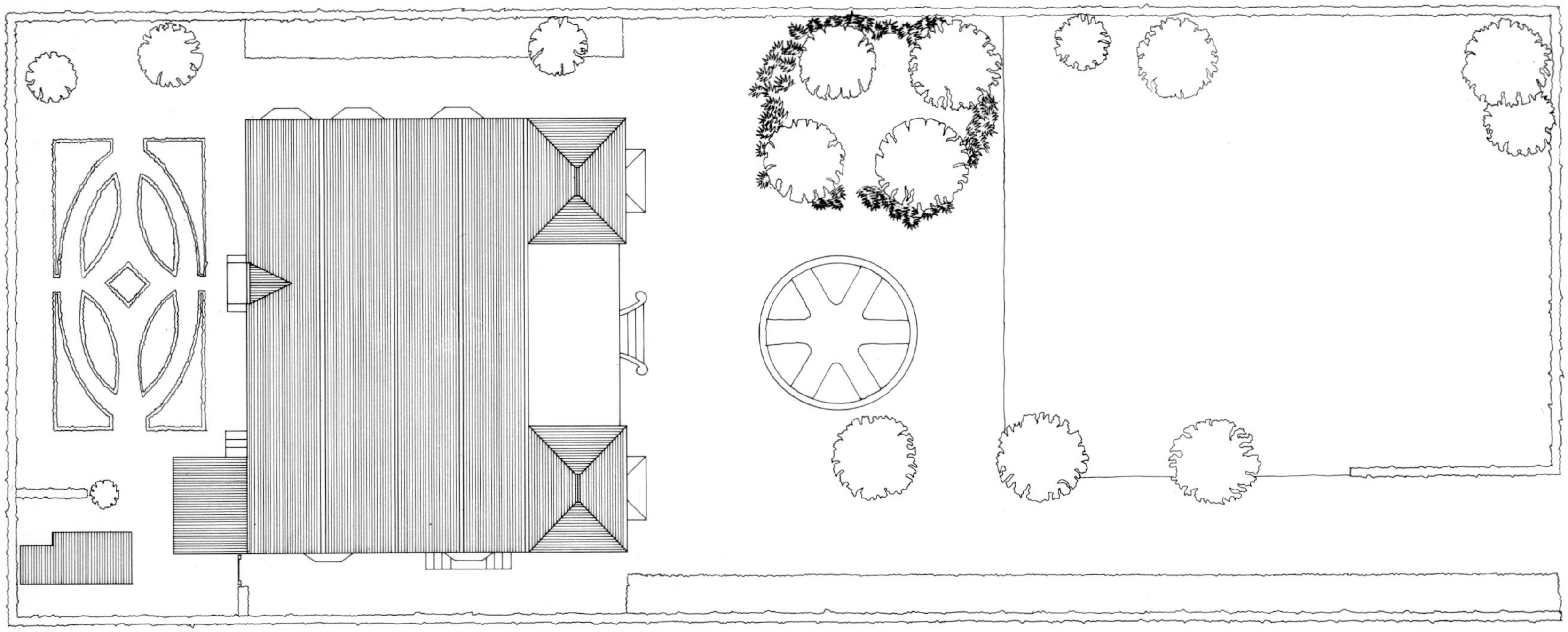

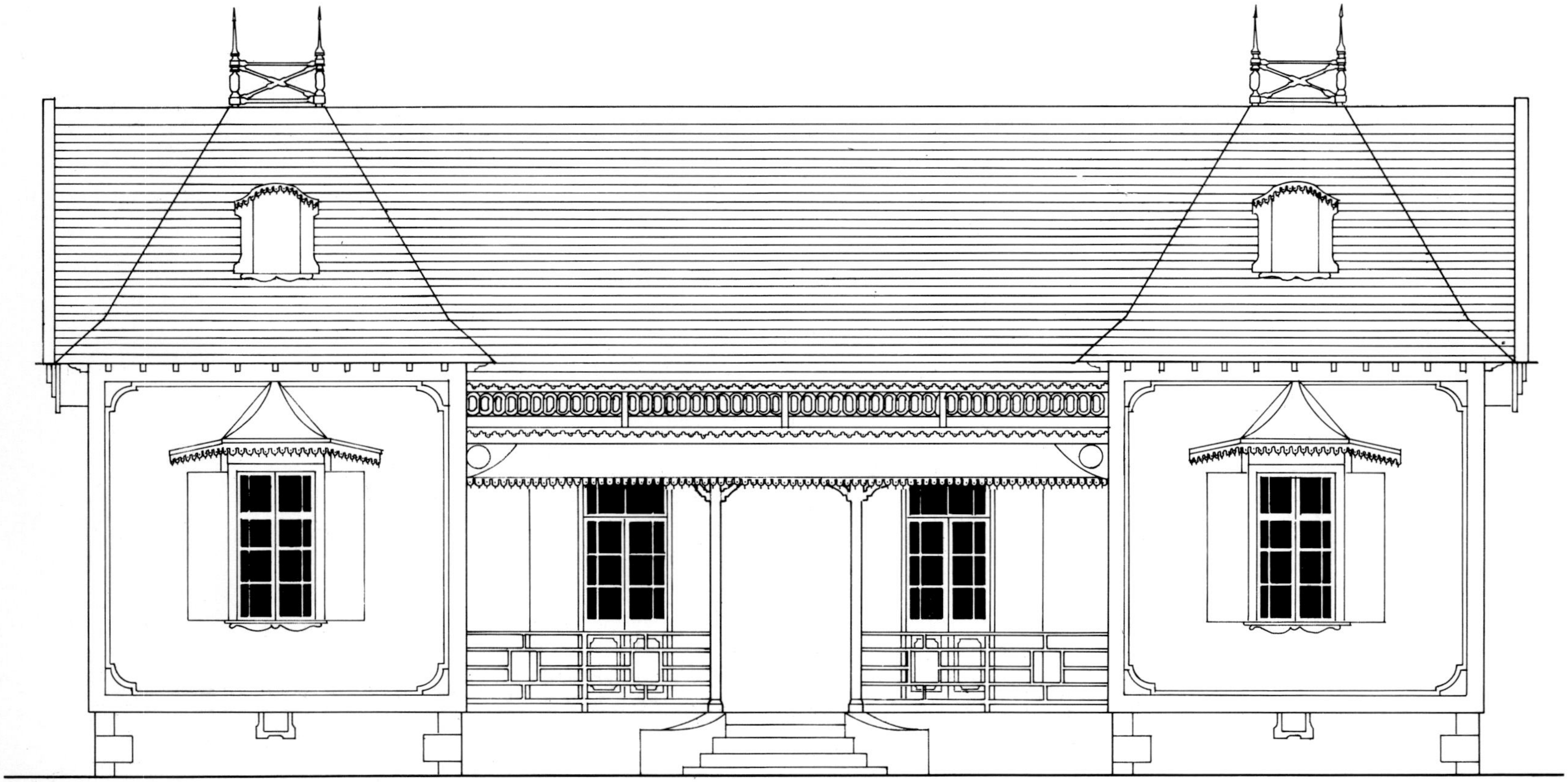

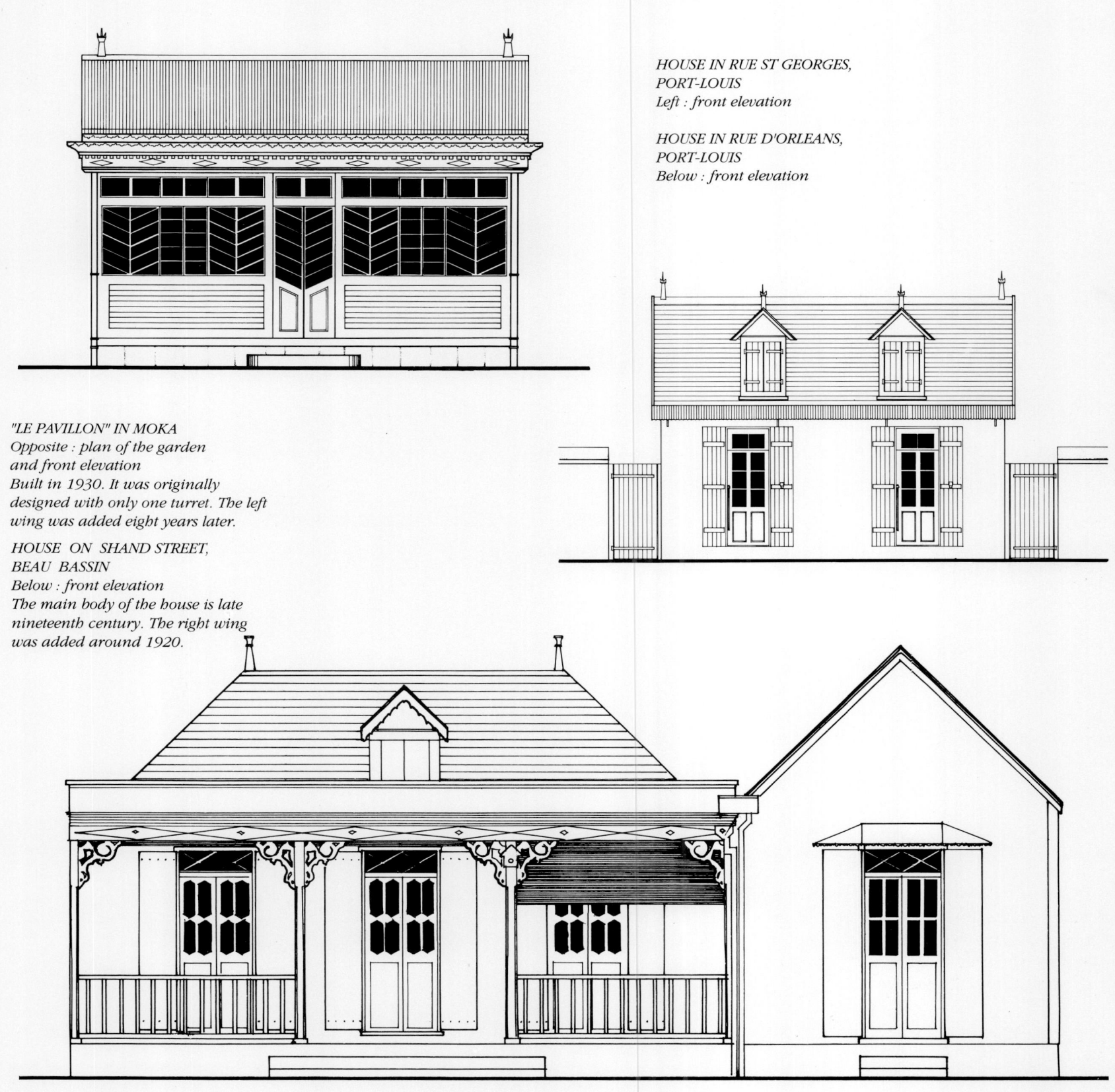

HOUSE IN RUE ST GEORGES,
PORT-LOUIS
Left : front elevation

HOUSE IN RUE D'ORLEANS,
PORT-LOUIS
Below : front elevation

"LE PAVILLON" IN MOKA
Opposite : plan of the garden
and front elevation
Built in 1930. It was originally
designed with only one turret. The left
wing was added eight years later.

HOUSE ON SHAND STREET,
BEAU BASSIN
Below : front elevation
The main body of the house is late
nineteenth century. The right wing
was added around 1920.

THE LAST BASTION OF CHARACTER 1930-1960

Alas, with the growing popularity of concrete as a building material, wooden architecture gradually fell into disfavour and would have completely disappeared were it not for the popular dwelling.

Compared, to the grander residences, its proportions are modest. Nonetheless, it features all the elements of Mauritian style. In particular, there are three characteristics which help to place it in a category of its own: firstly, corrugated iron is essential; secondly, the classical colours are replaced by vivid shades which reflect the Mauritian love of "Chazalian" colours; and, lastly, the strong symmetry of the large houses is not necessarily respected. The end result is often more picturesque than that of the more imposing counterparts.

In spite of its small size, the verandah is still used as the reception area and thus becomes the heart of the house, where people actually live. The bedrooms are generally arranged symmetrically and laterally in relation to the verandah.

The kitchen is usually situated at the rear of the house in a separate structure, just as in the large houses of yesteryear.

The traditional houses of Mauritius are fast disappearing; their survival is threatened by unrestrained urban culture. Let us hope that this book will help in rallying the whole population of Mauritius to preserve this invaluable part of its national heritage. At a time when environment is a subject of public concern, we sincerely hope that the authorities will not hesitate to adopt any new legislation that will stop the process of destruction : "...for a house that has braved the ages commands our respect. It captivates our soul..." (Jean-Louis Pagès, *Maisons traditionnelles de l'Ile Maurice*)

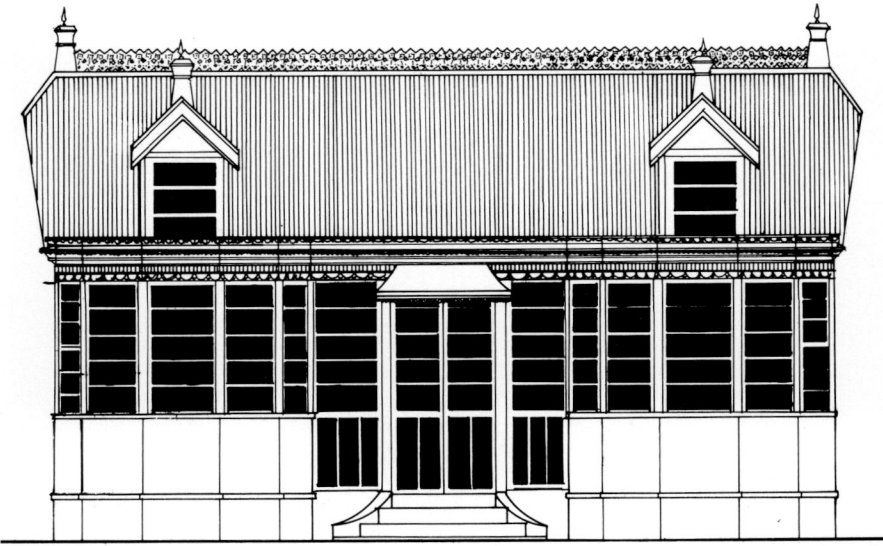

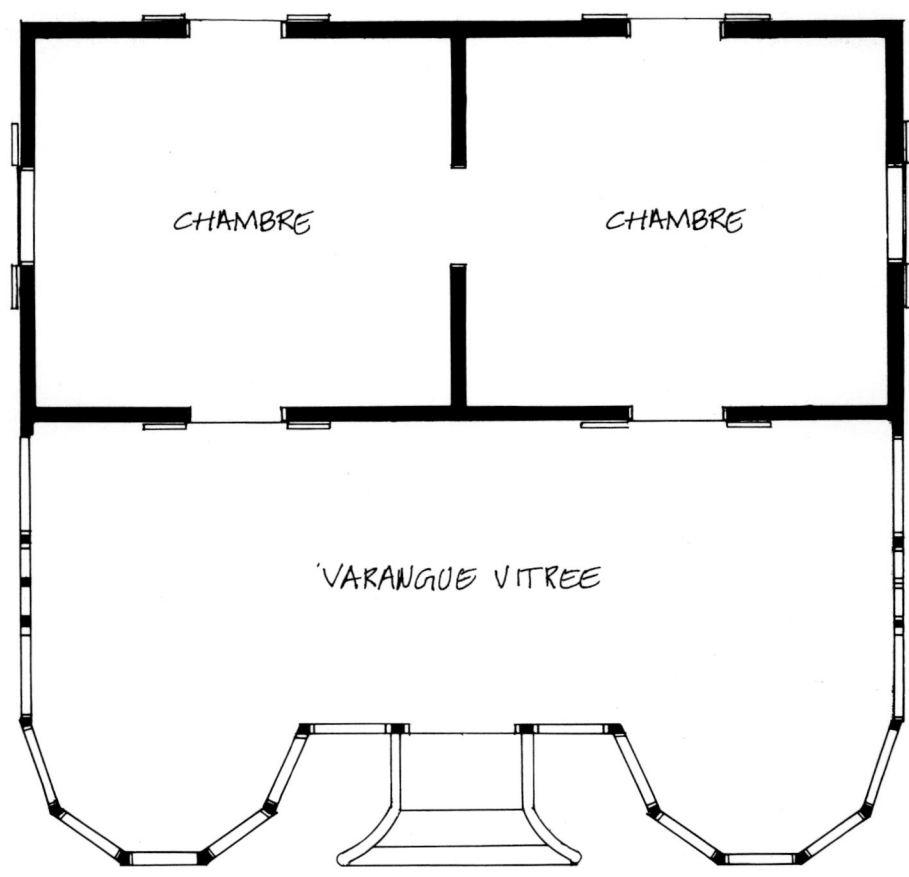

HOUSE IN MELROSE
Front elevation and plan
Built in 1958 by the Woozeer family.

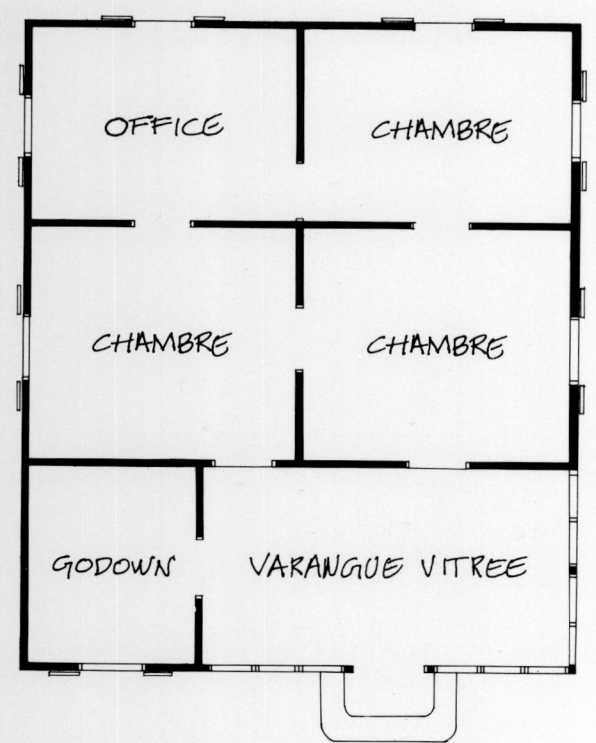
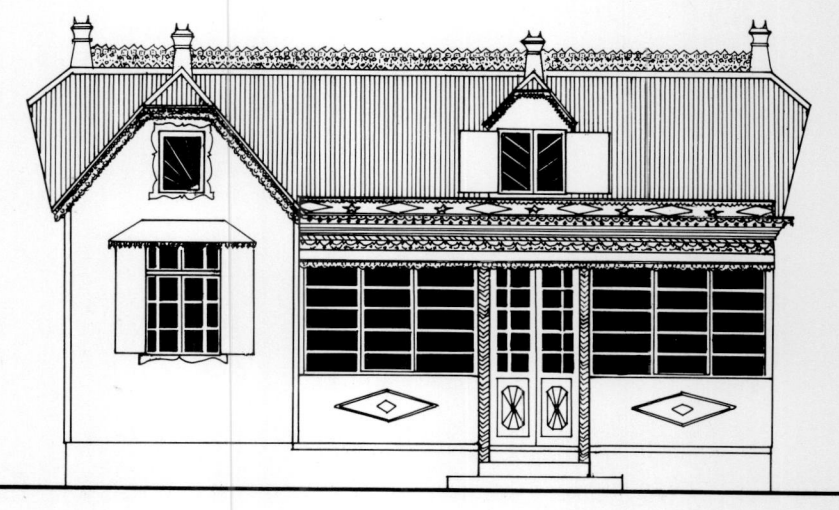

HOUSE IN TROU D'EAU DOUCE
Above : front elevation and plan
Built in 1958 by Mr Beejmohun.
Seriously damaged by Cyclone
Firinga (28 January 1989), the house
is scheduled for demolition.

HOUSE IN OLIVIA
Below : front elevation
Built around 1950 by Mr Patpur and
still occupied by the same family.

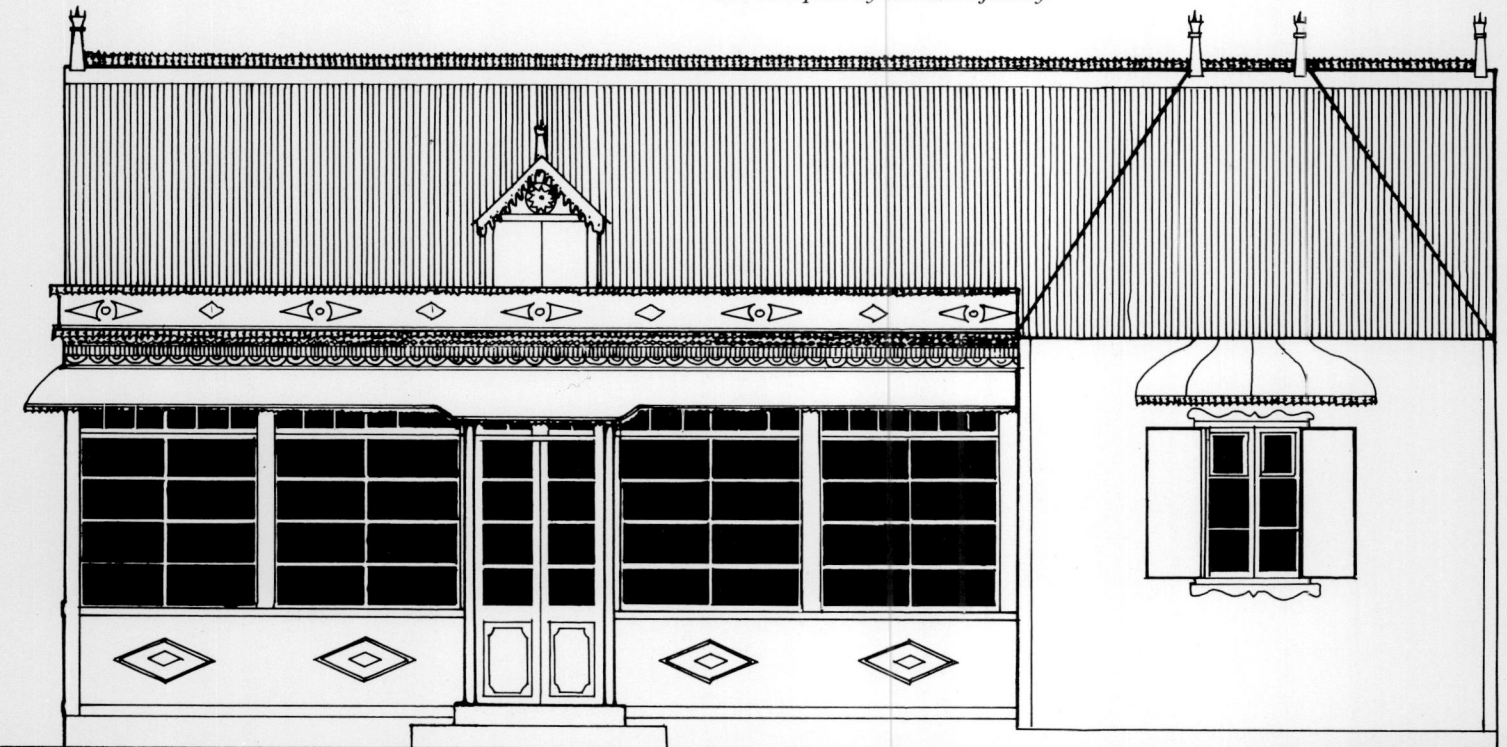

Château de Senneville, Curepipe
Damaged by the cyclones Carol and Gervaise, dismantled around 1976

'GONE WITH THE WIND'

Maison de Monsieur Ferdinand Desmarais, Quatre Bornes
Dismantled in the fifties

Château Candos, Candos
Demolished in 1986

Demeure Corbeyrier, Curepipe
Built in Port-Louis in 1918, dismantled and rebuilt in Curepipe

Le Clos Joli, Moka
Demolished in 1986

Villa Surprise, Curepipe
Dismantled after Cyclone Carol in 1960

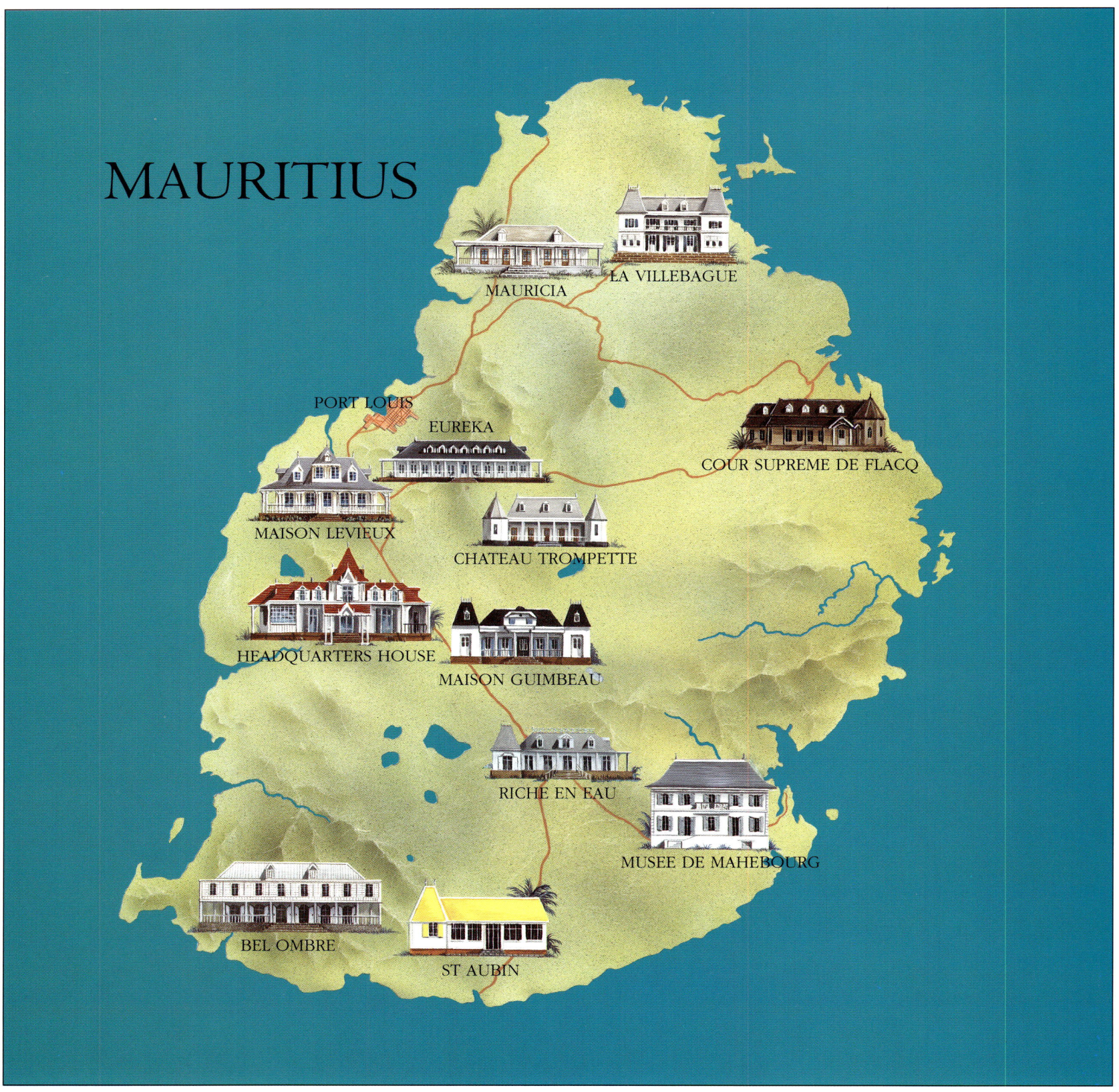

GLOSSARY

Argamasse: usually refers to the flat roof of the verandah; also refers to the mixture used to coat these roofs. There are numerous recipes for this mixture. Lime is the basic ingredient, but a surprising variety of other ingredients may be added.

Auvent: an overlang or canopy above a door or window; it protects the interior from both sun and rain.

Boutique: general grocery shop, usually owned and run by the Chinese.

Campement: a typical Mauritian term for a seaside bungalow. Originally applied only to the ravenala huts where families spent the summer months, the term is now used to describe any modern seaside cottage.

Case: a small house, or cabin, usually made of wood.

Chalis: polished cement floor used on the verandah and within the house and usually painted red.

Chassé: private land given over to deer hunting.

Chazal, Malcolm de (1902-1981): a Mauritian naïve painter.

Défriché: a plantation, literally an area of tropical forest that has been cleared.

Jardin d'hiver: literally winter garden, but comparable to a conservatory.

Ravenala: the central veins of the ravenala leaf are used in the construction of campements. The ravenala, popularly known as "travellers tree" originates from Madagascar.

Roche carri: cut stone on which spices are crushed. An indispensable part of the kitchen in any Mauritian home.

Season: winter months traditionally spent at the seaside.

Upper plateau: rising steeply from the coast, the elevation of the plateau varies from 200 to 700 metres; its coolness is much appreciated during the summer months.

BIBLIOGRAPHY

ECONOMY AND GEOGRAPHY

PADYA B M, Cyclones of the Mauritius Region (Met Off Mauritius, 1972)

PATURAU Maurice, Histoire Economique de l'Ile Maurice

HISTORY

ADOLPHE Harold and LAGESSE Marcelle, l'Hôtel du Gouvernement (1973)

BARNWELL P J, Visits and Despatches 1598-1948 (1948)

DE SORNAY Pierre, Ile de France, Ile Maurice (1950)

DUCRAY C G, Histoire de la Ville de Curepipe ; Notes et Anecdotes (1941)

FELIX J E, The Historical Monuments of Mauritius (Colony of Mauritius, Education Department, 1958)

JERNINGHAM H E H, GMG Lieut Governor of Mauritius and Dependencies, cyclone of April 29th in Mauritius, Pamphlets, Volume 124 (1892)

JESSOP A, A History of the Mauritius Government Railways, 1864-1964 (1964)

LAGESSE Marcelle, La recette de l'Argamasse (La Gazette des Iles de la Mer des Indes, Janvier 1987)

LE JUGE DE SEGRAIS René, Souvenir de Segrais et de Mongoust (1936)

MAC MILLAN A, Mauritius Illustrated Historical and Descriptive, Commercial and Industrial Facts, Figures and Resources (W H & L Collingbridge, London, 1914)

NEWTON Robert, Le Réduit 1748-1960 (1960)

PAGES J L, Maisons traditionnelles de l'Ile Maurice (Editions de l'Ocean Indien, Ile Maurice, 1978)

ROUILLARD G, Histoire des Domaines Sucriers de L'Ile Maurice, 1964-79 (The General Printing and Stationary Company Ltd, Mauritius)

TOUSSAINT A, Port Louis, Deux Siècles d'Histoires 1735-1935 (La Typographie Moderne, Port-Louis, 1936)

TRAVEL ACCOUNTS

BARTRUM Lady A, Recollections of Seven Years Residence at Mauritius; or the Isle of France; by a lady (1838)

BACKHOUSE Alexander, A Narrative of a Visit to the Mauritius (1844)

BEATON Rev P, Creoles and Coolies: or Five Years in Mauritius (Nisbet, 1859)

BOYLE CJ Far away, or sketches of scenery and society in Mauritius (1867)

ST PIERRE Bernardin de, Voyage à l'Ile de France (Amsterdam, 1773)

ST PIERRE Bernardin de, Conseil à un jeune colon de l'île de France (Amsterdam, 1818)

MILBERT M G, Voyages pittoresques à l'île de France (1812)

MOUAT F J, Rough notes of a trip to Réunion, the Mauritius and Ceylon with Remarks on their Eligibility for Indian Invalid (Calcutta, 1852)

Journal of five months Residence in Mauritius by a Bengal Civilian

(Calcutta, 1838)

A late official Resident, An account of the island of Mauritius and its Dependencies (1842)

THESES; UNPUBLISHED DOCUMENTS

DESMARAIS Pierre, A Study of Colonial Houses in Mauritius (1960)

DESVAUX DE MARIGNY Isabelle, The Colonial House in Mauritius (1980)

LAGESSE Henriette, The Traditional Colonial Architecture of Mauritius (Cambridge University, 1986)

LAGESSE Pierre, The Creole House of Mauritius, 1730-1890 (Cambridge University, 1959)

GENERAL REFERENCES

LA RÉUNION

Etudes Préliminaires sur l'habitat traditionnel dans le département de la Réunion (Ministère de la Construction et de l'Urbanisme, 1963)

DELCOURT J F, Regards sur l'architecture à St Denis, Ile de la Réunion (Direction Dept de L'Equipement Groupe d'Etudes et de Programmation)

VAISSE C, HENNEQUET F, BARAT C, AUGEARD Y, Cases cachées (Editions du Pacifique)

WEST INDIES

SLESIN S, CLIFF S, BERTHELOT J, GAUME M, ROZENSZTROCH D, l'Art de Vivre aux Antilles (Flammarion, 1986)

BERTHELOT J, GAUME M, Caribbean Popular Dwelling Exhibition, Centre Georges Pompidou (Perspective Creole, 1983)

EDWARDS J D, Cultural Traditions and Caribbean Identity; The Question of Patrimony; The Evolution of Vernacular Architecture in the Western Caribbean (Center for Latin American Studies, University of Florida, 1980)

USA

OVERDYKE Darrel W, Louisiana Plantation Houses. Colonial and Ante-Bellum

TOLEDANO, DITTREDGE EVANS, CHRISTOVITCH, The Creole Faubourgs. History by Samuel Wilson Jr, (New Orleans Architecture, Vol IV, Pelican Publishing Co, Gretna, 1974)

INDIA

KING A D, The Bungalow: the Production of a Global Culture (Routledge and Keegan Paul, 1984)

POTT Janet, Bungalows of Bangalore

AUSTRALIA

PAYNTER J, The Australian Verandah (Architecture in Australia, Vol 93, June 1965)

EUROPE

MIGNOT Claude, L'architecture au XIXe siècle (Editions du Moniteur, 1983)

ACKNOWLEDGEMENTS

We would like to thank all those who offered advice, enthusiasm and the permission for their houses to be included in this book. Special thanks to Guy Rouillard, Maurice Paturau, Jean-François Desvaux de Marigny, Philippe Valentin, Pierre Lagesse, Bernard Boullé for his help in translation, Tristan Bréville for the loan of photographs from the Museum of Photography, Guillemette de Spéville for her documents concerning Malcolm de Chazal, Marc Daruty de Grandpré for his drawings of Curepipe Town Hall and Guido A Rossi for the aerial photograph on page 63. Thanks also to Air Mauritius, the Ministries of Education and Tourism, and the hotel chains, Beachcomber, Sun International, Hotel PLM Méridien and Club Méditerannée. The photographer is especially grateful to Jacqueline Rabot for her invaluable help and advice.

All the exterior photographs were taken on Kodachrome 64 ASA and the interior ones on Ektachrome 100 ASA. The photographer used Nikon equipment.